# GRACE
# // TRUTH

## 1.0

Five Conversations
Every Thoughtful Christian Should Have
About Faith, Sexuality & Gender

—SECOND EDITION—

by DR. PRESTON SPRINKLE

THE CENTER FOR
FAITH, SEXUALITY & GENDER

# Contents

A Small Group Leaders Guide for Grace/Truth 1.0
is available as a download,
free at www.centerforfaith.com.

# Welcome!

Welcome to our conversation about faith, sexuality and gender! Whether you're new to this topic or have read many books on it, I pray that the next few weeks of conversation and study will be fruitful and rewarding.

Please note: This book is designed to be read alongside the *Grace/Truth 1.0* videos. If you're a leader, please make sure you have the videos, which are available for free on Right Now Media, or for purchase on DVD or through Vimeo (http://tinyurl.com/buyGrace-Truth1-0). And all *Grace/Truth* books and DVDs are only available from our online store (store.centerforfaith.com) and not from other retailers. We recommend that each member of the group read each portion of the book before the meeting. Then, at your meeting, you should watch the videos together before working through the questions. If you're going through the *Grace/Truth* experience by yourself (apart from a small group), then we still recommend (1) reading each conversation in the book, (2) watching the corresponding video, and (3) working through the questions.

Also, the book you're currently holding is the second edition of *Grace/Truth 1.0*. I've made a few changes in the second edition, but even if some in your group are reading from the first edition, it shouldn't be a problem for your discussion together. Most of the updates in the second edition are minor. The only place where I made extended changes are in the middle portions of conversation 3. My main points are still the same, but I've introduced some different arguments to support those points.

The ideas included under the terms faith, sexuality, and gender are many, and there's no way we can tackle them all in five weeks. To be clear, the primary focus of this study is on lesbian, gay, bisexual, and transgender (LGBT) people and what the Bible says about their experience. (This study will focus on LGB while *Grace/Truth 2.0* will focus more on the T.)

Some of you may have personal interest in the subject: Your son or daughter is gay, you have LGBT+ friends, or perhaps you are wrestling with your own gender identity or sexual attraction.

On the other hand, some of you may wonder why this topic warrants its own five-week conversation. After all, only a small percentage of the population (about 4 percent) identifies as LGBT+.

That statistic is sort of true. But only *sort of*. While only 4 percent identify as LGBT, about another 5 percent wrestle with their sexuality or gender identity on some level. This, of course, affects their mothers, fathers, brothers, sisters, friends, neighbors, and coworkers, which brings the percentage up to about 25 percent of the population who are deeply affected by this conversation.

And that's not all.

One of the main reasons young people are leaving the church is over how Christians have mistreated or failed to love LGBT+ people. My friend Bill Henson has trained more than fifty thousand Christian leaders to navigate questions of faith and sexuality. Over and over, leaders tell him that *how Christians talk about LGBT+ people is intrinsically related to whether younger straight people want to have anything to do with Jesus*. In fact, Bill has confidently concluded—and many other pastors I've talked to agree—that the evangelical church is about to lose an entire generation of Christians over how it has handled (or mishandled) this conversation. Younger people need to be shown a better way—the way of grace and truth. The way of Jesus.

One way or another, most Christians are affected by this conversation. And that's why this study might be one of the most important faith conversations you have this decade—or even the next.

## Grace/Truth 1.0 and 2.0

*Grace/Truth 1.0* is written primarily for Christians who believe in the authority of the Bible. You can think of it as a "Sexuality and Gender 101" guide that talks about language, relationships, and what the Bible says about marriage and same-sex relations. We'll emphasize two main themes in this study: One, LGBT+ related questions are not just about *issues*; they're about *people*. Two, we can have confidence that the traditional Christian marriage ethic (one man and one woman) is indeed biblical.

Part two of *Grace/Truth* (2.0) is more of a 201 guide for Christians and dives deeper into some complex aspects of this discussion. It wrestles with questions such as: *Were transgender people born into the wrong body? Are intersex persons neither male nor female? Why are some*

*Christians changing their view about marriage to include same-sex couples? Is gender fluid or stable?* And *how can churches effectively care for people struggling with their sexuality or gender?*

While *Grace/Truth 1.0* is a stand-alone study, and I think you'll learn a lot from it, I highly encourage you and your group to go through both 1.0 and 2.0. Even if your group can only commit to part 1, perhaps you personally can go through 2.0—if indeed you were challenged and blessed by 1.0!

A couple things to note as you're reading through this study. First, throughout our conversations, I'll reference various *pastoral papers* that go deeper into some points I make in this conversation, along with some episodes in the *Grace/Truth Podcast*—both of which you can access on the website of *The Center for Faith, Sexuality & Gender* (www.centerforfaith.com/resources-overview). The papers and podcasts are both optional. You can go through this study without accessing them. But for those who want more theological depth and practical guidance, you might find these studies helpful.

Second, you may have noticed that I've used the acronym LGBT+ a few times already. I'll explain what I mean by this in conversation 2. In short, I'm using the acronym to describe anyone who is attracted to people of the same sex or who experiences *gender dysphoria* (i.e., serious discomfort with their biological sex) or identifies with a gender different from their biological sex. The plus sign ("+") includes any other sexual minority or gender variant (meaning someone who doesn't express themselves as male or female) who doesn't quite fit the LGBT acronym (e.g., pansexual, asexual, gender fluid).

You should know that the LGBT+ acronym can be problematic for at least a couple reasons. First, it combines several very different identities, ideologies, and experiences into one single identity. It therefore runs the danger of failing to appreciate the diverse experiences of a diverse group of people. Many people who are "T" or included in the "+" are nothing like "LGB" people. Second, it's widely debated within evangelical Christianity whether Christians should identify themselves by their sexual orientation or gender identity. For instance, some say that Christians can struggle with "same-sex attraction" but should never identify as "gay."[1] I very much appreciate these concerns and will try to be sensitive to the different perspectives on these issues. In any case, when I use the acronym LGBT+, I'm using it in a very loose sense to describe anyone who simply doesn't fit the majority experience of being attracted to the opposite sex and comfortable with their biological sex. I'll explain this more in conversation 1.

If you already have a bunch of questions (or are confused!), please hang on until conversation 1.

With that in mind, I want you to meet my friend Jordan, whose story has reshaped reshaped how I think about people who are LGBT+. Okay, enough caveats. Let's get to know some people.

## WELCOME ENDNOTE

**1** For a discussion of these issues, see the series of posts on *The Center's* blog: https://www.centerforfaith.com/blog/gay-vs-same-sex-attraction-a-dialogue

# Dear Church: I'm Gay

His hands trembling and his face dripping with sweat, my friend Jordan waited anxiously in his car outside the church office.[1] He didn't want to go inside but knew he had to.

Jordan had recently come to grips with the fact that he was attracted to guys, and he'd even mustered up the courage to tell his pastor. But now he was about to go into a room full of church leaders and tell them that "I ... I am ... I'm ... g—." He could hardly say the words out loud even in the safety of his car. But in a few minutes, he would be saying those words out loud—to men he feared might not understand.

Jordan had just completed a year of college and had been heavily involved in helping lead the church's youth group. He had spent several years wrestling with his attraction to guys and concluded that God didn't want him to act on his attraction. Therefore, because of his unswerving allegiance to God's Word, Jordan had never touched another person romantically. No one at this church had known about his struggle.

When he entered the room, he was greeted with smiles. Palms still dripping with sweat, he decided to get it over with. "I know you all trust me and allow me to help out in church. So, I wanted to let you know that ... I mean ... I want to confess that, well ... I'm, sort of ... I'm ... I struggle with same-sex attraction. I'm ... I'm attracted to guys."

Silence.

"I thought he was a Christian," one leader whispered to another, as if he'd forgotten that Jordan was still in the room. A few feet away. With ears. That work.

"Jordan, when did you decide this?" one asked.

"Um ... when? What do you mean? I ... I didn't *decide* this. I don't *want* to be attracted to guys."

The leader continued, "You know, Jordan, what God thinks about homosexuality? He says it's a sin."

Jordan was taken aback. He didn't know what to say. The leaders seemed to assume that he was engaging in immoral sexual behavior. But Jordan was sexually pure. He was simply admitting his attraction to, not sexual activity with, other guys. *Is struggling with and resisting temptation a "sin"?* Jordan wondered. *Do these leaders never struggle with and resist sexual temptation?*

"Jordan, we can't condone someone with your lifestyle," another leader said with a look of concern.

*Lifestyle?* Jordan thought. *I haven't even touched another person romantically. What does "lifestyle" even mean?*

Before Jordan could respond, another leader added, "And what about our children? I mean, we can't have you working with our children!"

Jordan felt sick to his stomach. He didn't know how to respond. "Um … sir, I … I don't struggle with wanting to have sex with children. I'm gay, not a *pedophile.*" But the distinction between homosexuality and pedophilia seemed to sail right past the leaders.

As Jordan sat through the rest of the rather brief meeting, he felt dehumanized and misunderstood. The leaders had good intentions; they believed in God's Word and wanted Jordan to live a holy life. But misinformed assumptions about language ("we can't condone someone with your *lifestyle*") and people ("what about our children?") can crush someone's soul. The last thing Jordan remembers that night was heading to his car, locking the door, squeezing the steering wheel until his fingers turned white, and screaming away his pain.

## These Are Important ~~Issues~~ People!

My heart breaks whenever I think about Jordan in that church office. Unfortunately, I've talked with a lot of LGBT+ people, and almost all of them have similar stories of being made to feel less than human. I could fill this entire book—and several others—with stories similar to Jordan's, but let me share with you a "real time" message I literally *just* received through Facebook. It's from a young kid I've never met who read one of my books. We'll call him Joey. This is what he said:

> Hi. My name is Joey. I read your book *Living in a Gray World* and I'm struggling with same-sex attraction. I was wondering if you could help me cope with a problem at school. Well, I don't know where to begin. My so and so friend told the bus driver that I'm gay and things went south quickly. First, he moved all the boys forward and me to the

back of the bus. When I asked why he said "I may be a Christian, but I won't have an abomination sit next to the rest of my kids I need to get home. I don't need you doing stuff with them." The word got around school and now I can't go 23 steps without being looked upon like I grew a tail or being called f*g. And I'm scared to talk to my pastor. (Yes, I go to church.) I was wondering if you could help me.[2]

For the bus driver, homosexuality was some issue that needs to be confronted and resisted. It's a threat to his religion, and it needs to be crushed. But instead of actually crushing evil, the bus driver crushed a young boy created in God's image.

There's nothing in a Christian sexual ethic that allows us to dehumanize other people.

Jordan and Joey are only two of many LGBT+ people who have shown me that discussions about sexuality and gender should always be seen as closely connected to the actual people we're talking about. Homosexuality is not just an issue. Transgender people are not issues. The thirteen-year-old student in your youth group who's secretly contemplating suicide because he experiences unwanted attraction to boys and desperately wishes he would become attracted to girls—he's not an issue. He's an image-bearing human, crafted and cared for by his Creator.

In order to focus on people, we have to get rid of the stereotypes. Despite what you may see in the media or read about in the news, not all LGBT+ people are the same. As a straight man who grew up in a conservative Christian church, I used to believe the stereotypes. Effeminate men. Masculine women. Promiscuous people who march in pride parades wearing feathers and leather G-strings. But then I did something that changed my life.

I got to know several LGBT+ people and listened to their stories.

That's it. No agenda. No ulterior motive. I just wanted to connect closely with the "topic" I was studying. And it—or they—changed my life. Please note: My theology didn't change. I still believe that marriage is between a man and a woman and all sex outside of marriage is a sin. But my heart was changed. I began to love and truly enjoy all my new friends—some of whom you'll get to know when you discuss this conversation at the next gathering.

LGBT+ people are not all the same. I've met gay people who are trying to follow Jesus and gay people who want nothing to do with Jesus. Some of my gay friends are committed to celibacy because they believe gay sex is a sin; other gay friends are married to people of the opposite sex—and yet they are still gay. I know non-Christian gay people who are against gay marriage, and kids raised by gay parents who are pro-LGBT+ but against same-sex couples adopting kids. There are loud and proud LGBT activists, and silent and scared kids in your youth group struggling with their sexuality. One non-Christian gay man I know says he doesn't resonate with the gay community and would never march in a pride parade. He's not really into all that political gay stuff—even though he's gay. There are lesbians who think that transgender ideology is destructive and morally wrong, while other lesbians find comradery with transgender people. Some people who struggle with their gender reject a transgender identity, while others embrace it. As one psychologist said: "If you've met one transgender person, you've met ... one transgender person."

But then I did something that changed my life. I got to know several LGBT+ people and listened to their stories.

It's simply wrong and naïve to talk about "those gay people" or "the LGBT community" as if they're all the same. Not all LGBT+ people are alike. We have to take our stereotypes, fold them up, throw them in the trashcan, and then get to know *actual* LGBT+ people before we can think clearly about this issue. Because it's not just an issue. It's people.

# Sticks and Stones Will Break Your Bones— and So Will Words

One of the best ways to humanize this conversation is to learn the right language.

There's a stupid saying we used to memorize: "Sticks and stones will break my bones, but words will never hurt me." That's a lie. Words can do great harm. Millions of people have been psychologically and emotionally damaged over something somebody said to them more than twenty years ago—and this goes for all people, not just LGBT+ people. Hurtful words drive people toward eating disorders, depression, and suicide. Words have the power to both hurt and to heal, to build up and tear down. And unfortunately, Christians have unintentionally (or sometimes intentionally) crushed LGBT+ people by abrasive, ignorant, or downright mean words and phrases.

So, let's talk about language, beginning with some simple definitions. In conversation 5, we'll talk about some words and phrases to avoid, and I address several others in *Grace/Truth 2.0*.

### Gay

The word *gay* simply describes someone attracted to the same sex and not to the opposite sex. Please note: People use this term in very different ways.

Some gay people believe that gay sex is totally fine, while others think it's a sin. In itself, *gay* doesn't mean "having gay sex" or "married to a person of the same sex." It just means "attracted to the same sex."

### Same-Sex Attraction (SSA)

*Same-sex attraction* (SSA) is similar to *gay*, but it's usually used by Christians who don't want to be identified by their sexual orientation. Put simply, SSA is almost always used by conservative Christians to describe *unwanted* same-sex sexual attractions.

However, some Christians use the term *gay* as shorthand to say they are attracted to the same-sex (even if they're not having sex). In other words, they use *gay* in virtually the same sense as SSA. Remember: *gay* is a broad term and can be used in different ways to mean different things.

### Transgender

This is an umbrella term for anyone who doesn't identify with, or feels some sort of discomfort with, their biological sex. (By the way, it's *transgender*, not *transgendered* with an -ed.) There's more to it than that, but we'll take a deeper look into all of this in *Grace/Truth 2.0*. Two basic points you need to understand for now: (1) *transgender* is not the same as *gay*. Gay refers to whom someone is *attracted to*, while transgender refers to the gender someone *identifies as*. And (2) if someone identifies as *transgender*, that doesn't necessarily mean they've had a sex change (i.e., sex reassignment surgery or hormone replacement therapy, or both). Some have but many haven't.

There are many other phrases and concepts in the gender discussion that we'll get to in *Grace/Truth 2.0*—gender fluidity, gender nonconforming, gender queer, and other nonbinary categories.

### LGBT+

This acronym stands for **L**esbian, **G**ay, **B**isexual, and **T**ransgender. As I mentioned before, I like to add a plus sign (+) at the end of it to include all the other letters that are sometimes attached to this (growing) acronym, such as **Q**ueer, **I**ntersex, **A**sexual, **P**ansexual, and many others.

In our conversations, I'll use LGBT+ as shorthand for people who are same-sex attracted, experience discomfort with their biological sex (e.g. gender dysphoria), or are simply "nonstraight." Depending on the context, I may use LGBT+ to refer to Christians who are *struggling* with their faith, sexuality, and gender, even if they don't choose to identify as gay, bisexual, transgender, etc. Not every person who experiences same-sex attraction or discomfort with their gender identifies as LGBT+. I get that. But if I use the phrase "same-gender loving persons, people who experience gender dysphoria, and other nonstraight persons," our conversation would be twice as long! So, for convenience, I'll just use LGBT+ as a shorthand for that longer phrase in quotes above.

### Affirming and Historically Christian

These are the common labels Christians use to describe what they believe about same-sex marriage. Those who are *affirming* (gay or straight) believe that sex difference (male and female) is irrelevant for the meaning of marriage; they therefore endorse the idea of same-sex "marriage." Those who are *historically Christian* (gay or straight) believe that sex difference is an essential part of what marriage *is* and therefore see the idea of same-sex marriage as a contradiction in terms. (If marriage is by definition a union between two sexually different persons, then same-sex marriage isn't a thing.) There are other terms used to describe the affirming view, such as: *revisionist, progressive*, or *liberal*. Other terms for the *historically Christian* view include *traditional, nonaffirming*, and *conservative*.[3]

Every one of these terms has some problems. I used to use the term *nonaffirming* to describe my view, but I no longer love this term (even though I used it in the first edition). There are many things I *affirm* about my gay friends (their courage, beauty, generosity, self-giving love, etc.). Even so, I believe that marriage is, by definition, a union between a male and a female and that all sexual relations belong within this covenant bond. I also don't love the term *traditional* to describe my view of marriage. I'll use it sometimes, but I don't want to give the impression that I'm blindly adhering to a particular sexual ethic simply because of some tradition. I don't like the label *liberal* to describe people who affirm same-sex marriage because some *affirming* people are actually somewhat conservative; they resist the *liberal* label.

For more thoughts on terms and phrases, see the *Grace/Truth* podcast "Why Language Matters in the LGBT+ Conversation."

So, without better alternatives, I generally use affirming and historically Christian to describe the different views.

// // //

Some of you may be annoyed that we're wasting all this time and energy on language. After all, isn't this just a cowardly attempt to be politically correct? Are we tiptoeing around overly sensitive people with our language?

If we're just trying to be politically correct, then yeah, I'm not interested in that. But using language correctly honors the people we're talking about—people created in God's image. Plus, this isn't the only conversation where language matters. If after an abortion a doctor said he simply "discarded a fetus," many of us would protest and say he "killed an innocent unborn child." My Jewish friends tell me that there's a big difference between the question "Are you *Jewish*?" and "Are you *a Jew*?" The latter term carries with it shades of antisemitism, even if the person saying it doesn't mean it this way. The fact is, language matters! We love people well when we use language that humanizes them, which is especially important in a conversation that has dehumanized so many people.

## Is Same-Sex Attraction a Sin?

Speaking of people, I want to return to my friend Jordan and talk about something incredibly important: same-sex attraction.

Whether you're gay or straight, sexual *attraction* is not the same as sexual *behavior* or sexual *lust*. *Lust*, by the way, is a "desire for (and perhaps the planning of) an illicit sexual liaison."[4] It's important to realize that while sexual lust and illicit sexual behavior are sins, sexual attraction is not. You can be attracted to someone and not lust after them. If a beautiful woman walks into a room, I'd be a bold-faced liar if I said, "Nope, not attracted to her." But hopefully I would not actively desire to have sex with her. That would be lust. Put differently, lust assumes a prior attraction, but not all attraction leads to lust.

The same goes for people attracted to the same sex. I don't believe the Bible teaches that simply being same-sex attracted is a morally culpable sin. It may be a *temptation* to sin, and if the attraction turns into lust, then it becomes sin. But the fact that Jordan is attracted to the same sex is not in itself a sin.

Some people disagree with me. They say that same-sex attraction is itself sin. But the Bible never says this.[5] In fact, look at what James says:

> Temptation comes from our own desires, which entice us and drag us away. These desires give birth to sinful actions. And when sin is allowed to grow, it gives birth to death. (1:13–14 NLT)

James says that desires may "give birth to sinful actions," but he doesn't say these desires *are* "sinful actions." Think about James's metaphor of childbirth. A woman (desire) may give birth to a child (sinful actions), but this means that the woman *is not* the child. They're different. In the same way, desires may give birth to sin, but the desires themselves are not sin. Same-sex attraction is one of these desires. It could lead us to sin—as could *opposite sex attractions*! But simply existing as a same-sex attracted person isn't itself a morally culpable sin.

That is, it's not a sinful action that someone needs to repent from. And apart from some very rare examples, same-sex attraction is unchosen and, often at least initially,

> For a thorough study of what the Bible says and doesn't say about same-sex attraction, please see the pastoral paper "Is Same-Sex Attraction a Sin?"

unwanted.[6] I personally have never met a gay person who woke up one day and said, "You know what? I think I'm going to be attracted to the same sex." What people *do* with their attraction—same-sex or opposite sex!— involves choices and could lead to sin. (And if anyone reading this study is without sin, go ahead and cast that stone.) But the attraction itself is not sin.

Understanding this might be one of the most important steps in learning how to love gay people better. Can you imagine how Jordan's elders would have responded if they had understood the difference between same-sex *attraction* and same-sex *sexual behavior*?

## Being Gay Is Not a Sin

Some conservative Christians say that "being gay is a sin." But when they say "gay," they typically mean sexual lust, gay sex, and affirming same-sex marriage. Again, however, the term *gay* simply means "attracted to people of the same-sex" and doesn't have to include details about a person's sex life or views about marriage. This means that *being gay is not in itself a sin, since same-sex attraction is not itself a sin.* Many of my gay friends are committed to celibacy *because* they love the Bible—yet they're still gay. Some of my gay friends are married to people of the opposite sex (often called a "mixed orientation marriage") and believe in a traditional Christian sexual ethic, and they still identify as gay. Are they in sin for "being gay?" How are they sinning? And if you think that simply being same-sex attracted is a morally culpable sin, then what would repentance look like? Becoming straight?

I can't tell you how many people have been damaged by the statement "Being gay is a sin." A kid comes out to her parents and says she's gay, and her parents flip out and accuse her of living in sin—just because she said she's gay. Sticks and stones will certainly break your bones, but words used wrongly will crush your soul.

If same-sex attraction is not a sin, and *gay* means "to be attracted to the same sex," then being gay itself is not a sin.

This is also why the term *anti-gay* is a horrible description of the traditional Christian view of marriage. It never fails, whenever I speak on this topic—people almost always think in terms of two different views: the anti-gay view and the pro-gay view. They ask me which one I hold to and I say neither. If *gay* means "attracted to the same sex" and is used to describe *people*, then as a Christian, I could never be against *people*. No way. Jesus wasn't against people, and as a follower of Jesus, I'm *for* people. And since same-sex attraction (i.e., being gay) itself is not a sin, I'm not anti-gay. I'm actually *pro-gay*. I'm *pro-gay* in the sense that *I am for gay people and I want God's best for them and believe they can fully follow and honor God while being gay*. Because same-sex attraction (being gay) itself is not a sin.

So, can you be gay and be a member of a church?

Yes.

Can you be gay and serve on the worship team?

Yes, of course.

Can you be a gay pastor?

Absolutely.

In no way am I saying that *everyone* who identifies as gay can be a pastor. I don't believe that anyone who's living a sexually immoral life should be a pastor—gay or straight. But I know several gay (same-sex attracted) pastors who believe in and follow a biblical, Christian sexual ethic and a traditional Christian view of marriage. They're attracted to the same sex, but they believe that same-sex lust and same-sex sexual behavior is sin.

Simply being gay is not a morally culpable sin. But having sexual relations with someone of the same biological sex is sin. We'll see why in conversations 3 and 4.

## Can't They Just Pray It Away?

This leads to our final question: Can gay people just pray it away? Or—if a Christian still experiences same-sex attraction, does this mean they haven't prayed hard enough?

Several *nonaffirming* gay Christian writers have compared their same-sex attraction to a disability, and I find this comparison to be helpful.[7] Many Christians have been crushed by the assumption that if they're still gay, they haven't prayed hard enough, fasted long enough, or read the Bible as frequently as they should. Yet we don't place the same expectations on other people who experience a physical or mental disability. We don't tell blind people they haven't prayed hard enough since they're still blind. We don't tell physically disabled people that if they just read their Bible more, they'd get up and walk. We also shouldn't assume that the reason gay Christians are still attracted to the same sex is that they just haven't tried their hardest to get rid of it.

> The good news isn't "God can make you straight," but "God can make you holy."

Or take the example of an alcoholic. (I'm always wary of using analogies, since they're never exact. When I use them, I'm only trying to compare certain elements, not make a one-to-one correlation.) There's a reason alcoholics still say they're alcoholics even if they haven't had a drink in twenty years. It's because the desire to drink is always there, even if they don't act on it. I think we'd applaud an alcoholic for being twenty years sober; we wouldn't (or shouldn't!) say, "Well, if you'd just pray harder, you'd have no desire to drink."

Can God give sight to the blind and snuff out an alcoholic's desire to drink? Of course. But for whatever reason, this isn't how God typically works. (That's a whole other discussion.) So we shouldn't blame gay Christians for not praying it away. The good news isn't "God can make you straight," but "God can make you holy."

## QUESTIONS FOR DISCUSSION

1. Circle or highlight which words Jordan's elders used that conveyed ignorance or misunderstanding on LGBT+ related issues. How might they have worded their statements/questions differently in a way that wouldn't have dehumanized Jordan?

2. How might Jordan's elders have responded differently if they'd understood that same-sex attraction isn't a sin?

3. Do you have any biblical or theological disagreement with the argument above that same-sex attraction (or being gay) is not a sin? What biblical evidence do you believe supports your view?

4. What questions do you have about the terms discussed above (gay, same-sex attraction, transgender, and so on)? Please be willing to discuss your questions with the group.

5. LGBT+ people aren't the only ones who have been victimized by people using language ignorantly. Have you personally experienced similar frustration and pain as a result of people using words wrongly to describe you? Please describe.

6. Would you attend a church that has a gay pastor, deacon, elder, or worship leader? Why or why not? As part of your response, make it clear what you mean by *gay*.

7. Do you agree that gay people can't be expected to just "pray it away?" Why or why not? Why do you think some people have believed gays could simply "pray it away?"

8. Some Christians grew up with negative feelings about gay people. In general, do you believe they got their negative feelings from the Bible? Or from their culture and family upbringing? Or both? Please discuss.

9. What idea surprised you the most after reading this conversation?

## CHAPTER ENDNOTES

**1** "Jordan" is a pseudonym for my friend. This story represents the gist of what happened in that meeting, although I've included phrases and scenes from other events in Jordan's life.

**2** For the record, I have not been able to verify Joey's story, but it does reflect other true stories I have heard.

**3** *Conservative* has too many political connotations and is often caught up with an entire conservative way of thinking, which may or may not be biblical. Some people see me as conservative because I believe the Bible. Others think I'm liberal because I don't read it in the Kings James Version. The word *conservative* is terribly subjective. Even the phrase *historically Christian* is problematic; it could signify that I sign off on every minor detail about the church's historical view of marriage. When I say *historically Christian*, I simply mean the church's historical belief that sex difference is part of what marriage is and that all sexual relationships outside this marriage covenant are sin.

**4** R. T. France, *The Gospel of Matthew, NICNT* (Grand Rapids: Eerdmans, 2007), 204. The same Greek word for lust (*epithymeo*) in Matt 5:27 is used in the Greek translation of Ex 20:17 (the ten commandments) to prohibit *coveting* your neighbor's wife. You can recognize that your neighbor's wife is attractive without actually coveting (or lusting after) her.

**5** Some people argue that Rom 1:24–27 says that same-sex attraction is a sin. However, Paul condemns sexual lust in the context of sexual behavior. He's not thinking of same-sex attraction as a temptation that's resisted. See further the pastoral paper "Is Same-Sex Attraction (or Being Gay) a Sin?," https://www.centerforfaith.com/resources?field_product_category_tid=1.

**6** For instance, Cynthia Nixon from the hit show *Sex and the City* says that for her, being gay is a choice: http://www.nytimes.com/2012/01/22/magazine/cynthia-nixon-wit.html. See also Brandon Ambrosino

from *The New Republic*, https://newrepublic.com/article/116378/
macklemores-same-love-sends-wrong-message-about-being-gay.

**7** For instance, Nate Collins, *All But Invisible: Exploring Identity
Questions at the Intersection of Faith, Gender, and Sexuality* (Grand
Rapids: Zondervan, 2017).

# Grace/Truth—The Jesus Way

As far as we know from Scripture, Jesus never explicitly mentioned homosexuality. We have no record of him encountering a gay couple asking him about gay marriage or same-sex relations. But I believe that Jesus still gives us a profound model for how to relate to those who have been shunned by religious people.

*In this conversation, I want us to reflect on Jesus' posture toward people viewed as socially unacceptable sinners.*

Some of these people were innocent victims, like lepers or widows. But others were entangled in all kinds of sin: tax collectors, drunks, adulterers, and other sexually immoral sinners. What we see is that when Jesus encountered these people, he always started with love and acceptance of the person—and this love and acceptance often led to repentance and obedience.

Starting a relationship with love and acceptance does *not* mean you don't care about obedience. Jesus had an incredibly high standard of obedience. One of his most famous (and longest!) sermons is the so-called Sermon on the Mount in Matthew 5–7. In it, Jesus says that lust is just as bad as adultery, vengeance is always wrong, and loving your enemy is always right. He condemns divorce, taking oaths, hypocrisy, and being anxious about the future. Jesus had a very high standard of obedience. He wasn't a pot-smoking hippie who affirmed everyone's behavior. He was a strict religious teacher who preached hard-hitting sermons.

For an in-depth look at Jesus' view of homosexuality, see the pastoral paper "Why Didn't Jesus Mention Homosexuality?"

Jesus had a very high standard of truth, yet he loved those who fell short of that standard. Jesus was the embodiment of *grace/truth*.

## The Sinner in the Tree

Consider his encounter with Zacchaeus (Luke 19:1–10). The crowds see Jesus coming and they swarm the road.

Jesus stops, scans the onlookers, and then looks up into a nearby tree and sees a man perched up on a branch so that he could see Jesus. Jesus knew who the man was: a chief tax collector. And he was hated by everyone.

Tax collectors were Jews who worked for the Roman empire—the dark side of the first-century force. Rome had conquered and occupied Israel through much war and bloodshed. They had become the oppressive overlords who ruled the land. If you live in America, it's hard to picture this (unless you're Native American). We haven't had anyone invade our country and take it over. But imagine that North Korea, Russia, or some other country conquered America and ruled the land. They parachuted into your city, took your stuff, and told you what to do and what not to do. (I'm getting flashbacks of watching *Red Dawn*.) And there's nothing you could say about it. Then imagine that your next-door neighbor went to work for this foreign country. His new job was to go door to door, take people's money, and give it to your new rulers.

> Jesus had a very high standard of truth, yet he loved those who fell short of that standard. Jesus was the embodiment of *grace/truth*.

So it is with Zacchaeus. He is committing political and religious treason right under your nose. Plus, tax collectors were known for living excessively immoral lives. They were greedy little extortionists who didn't have a moral bone in their bodies.

And so as Jesus gazes up into the tree, he notices a tax collector. But not just any tax collector. Zacchaeus was a *chief* tax collector, and he was *rich*. Not only was he an extortionist—he was a very successful one!

What do you, as one of the Israelites standing beside the road that day, expect Jesus to say? He could call Zacchaeus on the carpet and shame him in front of the crowd. "Come here, you little abomination! How dare you cheat and steal and lie! You better give back everything that you stole or I'm going to go all messianic on you!" Jesus could rub Zacchaeus's face in his many sins. He could confront. He could shout. He could grab him by his wee little ankles, turn him upside down, and empty his pockets of all his stolen money.

But what does Jesus say?

> Zacchaeus, come down immediately. I must stay at your house today. (Luke 19:5 NIV)

That's it. No rebuke. No shame. No MMA moves.
Nothing.

When Jesus says, "I must stay at your house today,"
he wasn't just looking for shelter. He was looking for
friendship. In Jesus' day, staying at someone's house
meant that you were friends with that person. That you
valued them, cared for them, and enjoyed being around
them. Only friends would stay at each other's house.
Enemies wouldn't cross the threshold of an enemy's
house.

But Jesus isn't Zacchaeus's enemy. He's his friend.

After Jesus enters Zacchaeus's house, the crowd goes
nuts! "Jesus has gone to be the guest of a sinner," they
grumble. But Jesus goes anyway. He cares more about
welcoming a sinner than pleasing the saints. Once he's
inside the house, you might expect Jesus to shut the
door, turn to Zacchaeus, and say, "Okay, look. I didn't
want to do this in front of everyone. But you've got some
serious issues. You're a liar, a cheater, and a thief. And if
you don't repent, you're going to hell!" But Jesus doesn't
say this—even though it's all true.

What does Jesus say?

Nothing.

He doesn't say a word.

He doesn't talk to Zacchaeus about his stance on extortion, nor does he march through the laundry list of Zacchaeus's sins. Jesus doesn't confront, nor does he rebuke. He simply accepts and loves.

Now look at Zacchaeus's response:

> Zacchaeus stood up. He said, "Look, Lord! Here and now I give half of what I own to those who are poor. And if I have cheated anybody out of anything, I will pay it back. I will pay back four times the amount I took." (Luke 19:8 NIrV)

Zacchaeus repents. He turns from his sin. He desires to be holy. And it wasn't Jesus' stance on extortion that motivated Zacchaeus's repentance. Rather, it was Zacchaeus's encounter with the unconditional acceptance of Christ.

Because sinners in need of grace can't obey God until they are first accepted by God. *Acceptance precedes obedience.*

## Jesus Begins with Love

When Jesus meets Zacchaeus, he begins with love. And this is the same pattern we see throughout Jesus' life. Whenever he meets people whom the religious elite thought were terrible sinners, Jesus first assures them that they are loved.

When Jesus meets a military leader of Rome—that oppressive empire ruling over Israel—he accepted and loved him. He could have destroyed his enemy, and all the religious people would have cheered him on. But instead, Jesus conquered the military leader with love. When the man asks Jesus to heal his servant, Jesus responds not with a sword but with grace (Matt 8:5–12).

The same goes for Matthew, another tax collector like Zacchaeus (Matt 9:9—13). Jesus sees "a man named Matthew sitting at the tax collector's booth" and says to him, "Follow me." Immediately, "Matthew got up and followed him" (Matt 9:9 NLT). As with his encounter with Zacchaeus, Jesus accepts Matthew without trying to lecture him into the kingdom.

We see the same pattern every time Jesus meets people viewed as socially unacceptable sinners by religious people. In the story of the prodigal son, the father who represents God "felt compassion, and ran and embraced" his sinful son *before* he knew that his son was repentant (Luke 15:20 NIV). Jesus declared to the woman caught in adultery, "Neither do I condemn you" *before* he said, "Go, and from now on sin no more" (John 8:11 ESV). Jesus forgave the many sins of a prostitute who was washing his feet without ever mentioning her sins (Luke 7:36–50).

Does this mean that Jesus affirmed everyone's sin? Of course not. Did Jesus care about obedience? Absolutely. Did Jesus care about truth? (Do I really need to answer this?) Whenever Jesus encountered people who were engaged in sin, Jesus showed love. He loved people *into* obedience. Why? Because *it's God's kindness that leads to repentance, not our repentance that leads to God's kindness* (Rom 2:4).

> Whenever Jesus encountered people who were engaged in sin, Jesus showed love. He loved people *into* obedience. Why? Because *it's God's kindness that leads to repentance, not our repentance that leads to God's kindness.*

# Gay Is the New Tax Collector

In many ways, Christians have treated gay people the same way that Pharisees treated tax collectors. And so Jesus' approach to tax collectors gives us a good model for how we are to embody the gospel toward gay people.

We have to be careful with this analogy though. gay people are actually nothing like tax collectors of the first century, so I'm not comparing gay people to tax collectors. Some of my gay Christian friends are incredibly moral, and even my non-Christian gay friends sometimes embody more virtues than some Christians I know. I'm only comparing how religious people *have viewed* the two. Ancient Jewish people treated tax collectors with scorn, ridicule, and shame. And many Christians have historically treated gay people the same: scorn, ridicule, and shame.

Religious people have viewed both tax collectors and gay people as socially unacceptable sinners.

But then there's Jesus—full of truth *and* grace. Perfectly gracious and perfectly truthful. Remember: Jesus has a very high ethical standard and deeply desires our obedience. The question is, Why does Zacchaeus obey?

He obeys because he was first accepted.

Certainly Jesus didn't approve of Zacchaeus's sinful life, and yet he didn't feel the need to address every sin in the man's life. "You know, Zacchaeus, we can be friends and all, but you have to first know where I stand on the issue of the tax-collecting lifestyle and the Roman agenda. And I guess I'll stay at your house, but you need to first give back all the money you stole." Jesus doesn't do that. Even though he desires Zacchaeus's obedience, he pushes obedience out the other side by first showing acceptance.

Some Christians have a hard time accepting gay people. Maybe that's because we think that if we show acceptance, then it will look as if we affirm same-sex relations. Jesus wasn't worried that his acceptance of Zacchaeus might somehow show that he was soft on sin.

Jesus didn't seem to care about his reputation. He only cared about loving sinners like crazy—*especially* the ones that religious people have a hard time accepting. In fact, Jesus had so many friends who were drunks and tax collectors and partiers that he developed his own reputation: "Here is a glutton and a drunkard," the religious people said of Jesus. "He's a friend of tax collectors and sinners" (Matt 11:19).

*Until Christians develop the reputation of being far too chummy with gay people, we fail to imitate Christ as we ought.*

*Acceptance* doesn't equal *affirmation*. That is, accepting someone's humanity doesn't mean that you approve of everything they do. Therefore, you should be eager to accept gay people *as people*, but this doesn't mean that you applaud their every act.

## Biblical Love

But some people don't agree. They think that you can't love someone unless you affirm everything they do. Have you ever run into this? If you try to help someone to stop sinning, or if you disagree with something they're doing, they turn around and say, "I thought you loved me!" This is pretty normal in the world's way of thinking. The assumption is that if you truly love someone, you will let them live however they want.

But this isn't biblical love. Biblical love isn't *based on* a person's holiness—if you do the right thing then I'll love you. But it does *seek* a person's holiness. Jesus said, "If you love me, keep my commandments" (John 14:15 ESV), and Paul said that love "does not rejoice at wrongdoing, but rejoices with the truth" (1 Cor 13:6 ESV).

Biblical love is unconditional. But that doesn't mean that such love doesn't care about obedience. I think this is why so many Christians are scared to love LGBT+ people too much. They fear that if they "accept" them, this means they "affirm" same-sex marriage. But Jesus never had this fear, and neither should we. Again, *acceptance doesn't mean affirmation*. Think about it.

Jesus hung out with prostitutes, but he didn't endorse prostitution.

Jesus hung out with tax collectors, but he didn't affirm extortion.

Jesus defended a woman caught in adultery, but he wasn't pro-adultery.

Acceptance doesn't have to mean affirmation. Biblical love *accepts* people as they are and then loves them into the people God wants them to be.

## LGBT+ People in the Church

The fact is, most LGBT+ people (83 percent) grew up in the church, but many ended up leaving the church. We'll explore this more in *Grace/Truth 2.0*. The fact is, most LGBT+ did *not* leave the church because of its theology of marriage and sexuality. They left because they were dehumanized.

For instance, Eric Borges was gay and raised in a Christian home, and he was dehumanized limb by limb by his peers at school. "My name was not Eric, but Faggot. I was stalked, spit on, and ostracized ... I was told that the inherent, very essence of my being was unacceptable." Even his Christian parents told him he was "disgusting, perverted, unnatural, and damned to hell."[1]

Ben Wood was a gay Christian teen who was active in his church. One day at youth group, his pastor shamed him in front of the entire group: "You all know ... that Ben is gay. Who here is comfortable being around him?" Then, "Do you understand that Ben is going to hell?" Ben was told that he could not attend the upcoming missions trip and that he didn't deserve to be part of the youth group. Ben was shamed, humiliated, and betrayed by other kids in the group who were pressured into agreeing with the youth pastor.[2]

Lesli Hudson-Reynolds struggled with her gender identity as a child. She was also passionate about following Jesus. But when she was a teenager, she was told that she was an "abomination," "un-savable," and "damned to hell." After hearing this, she thought, *I was ashamed that I was such an abomination to the God that I adored.* After going to the pastor for help—help for simply struggling with her gender identity—Lesli was ushered out of the church and invited to never come back again.

Tim Otto is a gay Christian and grew up as a missionary kid. He often struggled with his faith and sexuality—and still does. One night, Tim had sex with an anonymous man in the back room of an adult bookstore. Immediately after, he contemplated suicide. As he recalls: "I wish that somehow, rather than ending up in the arms of that anonymous man, I could have found myself in the arms of the church ... I wish in the church I had found myself loved."[3]

For more thoughts on the way of Jesus in the LGBT+ conversation, listen to the *Grace/Truth* podcast "The *Grace/Truth* way of Jesus toward LGBT+ people."

Fortunately, Tim didn't commit suicide that night. Shortly after, he found the love he was looking for—the love of other Christians who accepted him. Most of them believed that gay sex was sin, but they accepted Tim for who he was and created a safe place in the church where Tim could belong.

Likewise, Lesli was welcomed back into the church by a loving pastor who treated her like a human and not an abomination. This pastor believes that same-sex relations are sinful, but he also believes—as Jesus did—that *not* loving same-sex attracted *people* is sinful as well. Lesli is now a wonderful believer in Jesus.

Unfortunately, not every story ends on a positive note. One month after Eric Borges told his story on YouTube, he killed himself. Ben Wood also couldn't handle the loneliness and shame any longer. He also killed himself. These teens didn't end their lives because they were told that gay sex is wrong but because they were mocked, ridiculed, dehumanized, unwanted, and unloved. And there's nothing Christ-like about this. Jesus attracted many tax collectors and sinners to himself (Luke 15:1), and they didn't walk away wanting to kill themselves.

This is the *grace/truth* way of Jesus—to hold to a very high standard of obedience *and* to excessively love those who fall short of it. Being truthful means that we believe what God says about marriage and sex. Being gracious means we accept people for who they are, *as* they are, and love them into the obedience God calls us to. *Acceptance precedes obedience*.

## When Two Lesbians Walk into Your Church

I read a story a while back about two lesbians who decided to go to church one Sunday just to make

Christians mad.[4] "Let's just go for fun! We'll see how much we can push their buttons," Amy told her girlfriend. "I hear their motto is 'Come as you are,' I just want to prove that this means 'Come as you are … unless you're gay.'"

So Amy and her girlfriend went to church. Not to learn, but to provoke. They flirted in front of everyone, held hands, and made it very clear that they were lesbians. How did the church respond?

Amy recalls, "Instead of the disgusted looks of contempt we *expected*, people met eyes with us and treated us like real people." It's pretty cool how the church humanized this lesbian couple. But there's something Amy says here that makes my heart break.

The word *expected*.

"Instead of the disgusted looks of contempt we *expected*, people … treated us like *real people*." Amy and her girlfriend were shocked that these Christians treated them like real human beings and not monsters.

Why was this shocking? What else should they expect from a bunch of sinners saved by grace? How else should beggars, who have found bread, treat other beggars in search of bread?

*Expected.* They expected Christians to treat them like abominations, monsters, a subspecies of the human race. Instead, they were shocked that followers of Christ actually acted like Christ.

But Amy's story has a happy ending. She ended up breaking up with her girlfriend, but she kept coming back to church. The more she was accepted, the more she returned, and the more she returned, the more she was accepted.

> The more I listened and learned about the teachings of Jesus, the more I started to actually believe that God really did love me. I heard more and more about being His masterpiece, and in time, I actually started to believe it. The more I believed God actually could see something of value in me, the more I trusted Him.

Amy was accepted and loved. Unconditionally. And *that's why* she turned to God. Always remember: *Acceptance precedes obedience.* We can never obey God until we are first accepted by God. And we'll never experience acceptance by God until we are accepted by God's people.

## QUESTIONS FOR DISCUSSION

1. Describe in your own words the meaning of the phrase "acceptance precedes obedience."

2. If you have an LGBT+ friend or relative who grew up in the church, what was their experience like (if they wouldn't mind your sharing)? Please don't use names or disclose identities without permission.

3. Have you ever experienced someone's embodying the kindness of God, which led to your repentance? Maybe it was part of your conversation experience, or a time when you were in sin as a Christian and were turned back to God by someone else's kindness. Describe that experience.

4. This conversation focused on *not* beginning a relationship by confronting someone with their sin. Do you think there is a place for addressing someone else's sin early in the relationship? Why or why not?

5. Which of the two phrases do you like better and why?
   a. Love the sinner and hate their sin
   b. Love the sinner and hate your own sin

6. Most Christians are prone to emphasize either grace or truth in their relationships—especially with LGBT+ people. Which one (grace or truth) comes more naturally to you and why?

7. Why do you think Jesus never explicitly mentioned homosexuality? Do you think this means he didn't have an opinion about same-sex sexual relations? Discuss the reasons for your answers.

8. Do you think that Christians tend to condemn same-sex sexual sins more than heterosexual sins? If so, why do you think this is?

9. Discuss this statement: "If we're kind and welcoming to LGBT+ people, they may mistakenly believe that we have a gay-affirming theology."

10. If two lesbians walked into your church and showed public affection for each other, would they be met with disgusted looks or warm greetings? If the former (disgusted looks), what can you do to begin to change this culture? And if the latter (warm greetings), why do you think the church would receive them as such?

## CHAPTER ENDNOTES

**1** See Eric's testimony on YouTube, which was posted one month before he killed himself: https://www.youtube.com/watch?v=0Wy mBCOSB_c.

**2** Julie Hilliard Wood, "Shamed: How the UMC Contributed to My Son's Death," blog of Reconciling Ministries, December 10, 2013, https://www.rmnetwork.org/newrmn/shamed-how-the-umc -contributed-to-my-sons-death/.

**3** Tim Otto, *Oriented to Faith: Transforming the Conflict over Gay Relationships* (Eugene, OR: Cascade, 2014), 6.

**4** John Burke, "When Two Lesbians Walk into a Church Seeking Trouble," *CharismaNews*, March 13, 2014, http://www.charismanews .com/opinion/43109-when-two-lesbians-walk-into-a-church -seeking-trouble.

# What Is Marriage?

Imagine you have a friend named Kristy. You grew up together in church. She's now twenty-five and she came out as gay just two years ago. You've been trying to navigate the relationship ever since. Sometimes it goes well; other times it feels awkward—for both of you. You don't really talk about the fact that she's a lesbian, but one day she comes to you and says, "Megan and I plan to get married! You'll come to the wedding, right?"

You're not sure what to say, but your blank stare is already saying too much. You decide to speak, and the first thing that comes out of your mouth is the stock Christian response: "But Kristy, the Bible says you can't marry a woman. It only says you can marry a man."

"Where? Where does the Bible say, 'Thou shalt not marry someone of the same sex'? Show me!"

"Well," you say, "I mean … I'm not sure exactly where it says it, but I know it's there."

"Right," Kristy says. "Well, the Bible *never* actually says gay marriage is wrong. Conservative Christians just assume this, but it's not there. Besides, doesn't God want me to be happy? We were taught in church that God is love, and I can't imagine that a loving God would want me to marry someone I don't love, or not get married at all. Do you really expect me to stay single and lonely all my life?"

"God *is* love, but he is also clear about marriage being between one man and one woman for life."

"For life?"

"Yes, for life."

Kristy raises an eyebrow. "Didn't your brother Eddy, who had an affair and divorced his wife, end up getting remarried? Does the Bible say this kind of divorce is okay?"

You hesitate. "Well, no, it doesn't. But—"

"And you went to Eddy's second wedding, right? You even bought him and his new wife a gift. Wasn't that condoning his second marriage even though the Bible doesn't? And if you condone his marriage, which you said isn't biblical, then why wouldn't you bless me in my marriage—even though you don't think it's biblical?"

"But Eddy's divorce isn't the same as a gay marriage," you say.

"I'm not saying they're the same. I'm only saying that you supported one type of marriage which you just acknowledged isn't biblical, yet it sounds like you don't support mine. Why would you make an exception for Eddy but not for me? Sounds hypocritical."

Silence.

"In fact," Kristy goes on, "two deacons at our church have been divorced. No one is kicking them out of the church. It just seems like Christians are so selective in which types of marriages they condemn and which ones they celebrate."

If I can be honest, I think Kristy raises some very good questions. I know a lot of people who have been in dialogues almost identical to this one. By the end of our conversation, we'll be able to respond more thoughtfully and biblically in a dialogue like the one above, always seeking to embody that difficult, always messy, sometimes unclear, but oh-so-very-Jesus-like *grace/ truth* way.

## Two Different Definitions of Marriage

Defining marriage is the theological starting point for debates about same-sex marriage in the church. There's no point in arguing about some verses in Leviticus and Romans that prohibit gay sex if we don't first understand what marriage is.

In general, there are two different definition of marriage, which go something like this:

**1** Marriage is a lifelong union between two sexually different people.

**2** Marriage is a lifelong union between two consenting people.

The first definition rules out the possibility of something called "same-sex marriages," since, by definition, marriage *is* the union between two people of different sexes—male and female. If you think about it, even the phrase "male and female *marriage*" would be redundant, since marriage *means* the union between *male and female*.

This first definition is the historically Christian view. It's been held by all branches of Christianity for two thousand years. And today, it's still held by most Christians (and non-Christians) around the globe.

More recently, the second definition—that marriage is between two consenting adults *regardless of sex difference*—has blossomed in popularity among many western countries (the U.S., Canada, Europe, etc.). It's what's assumed in the famous 2015 Supreme Court decision to legalize same-sex marriage. After all, if sex difference is an intrinsic part of what marriage is (the first definition), then same-sex marriage isn't a thing. But if sex difference is not part of what marriage is (the second definition), then same-sex unions can be considered marriages.

So, before we even ask (or answer!) the question: *Can two people of the same-sex get married?* We have to first ask: *What is marriage?* In fact, there are three main questions that everyone should be able to answer before they give an opinion about same-sex marriage:

- First, what is your definition of marriage? That is, do you agree with the first or second definition above?

- Second, where did you get that definition from?

- Third, how does Scripture inform your definition of marriage?

These questions get to the absolute heart of the theological debate about same-sex marriage in the church. And here's what is truly shocking—many really smart people have formed their views about same-sex marriage *without ever asking or answering these three simple questions*. I've read whole books—several, actually—that argue for same-sex marriage in the church and yet never even raise the question: *What is marriage?*[1]

Here's how I would answer these three questions. The first one is easy: I agree with the first definition of marriage listed above. To expand on it a bit: *Marriage is a one-flesh covenant union between two sexually different persons (male and female) from different families, and God intends for sexual relations to take place within this marriage covenant.*

Where did I get this from? And how does Scripture inform this definition? I'm glad you asked! The short answer to both questions is: I get it from Scripture, and here's how.

## Sex Difference in Marriage

As I read Scripture, it seems rather clear that marriage is by definition the one-flesh covenant union between two sexually different persons. But don't just believe this because I believe it. Your faith should be in God and his Word, not in me. So let's take a look at Scripture and see what it says, starting with Genesis 1-2—the most foundational passage for understanding marriage.

Genesis 1 is a beautiful display of creational differences singing together in harmony. Unity among difference is an underlying theme. Heaven and earth, evening and morning, land and sea, day and night, light and darkness—*different* aspects of God's good creation playing *different* roles in broadcasting God's glory. Unity among difference. The climax of Genesis 1 is the creation of humanity in God's image as male and female:

> So God created mankind in his own image, in the image of God he created them; male and female he created them (Gen 1:27 NIV).

The creation of humanity as sexually different persons, "male and female," is woven into the fabric of God's creation account. And not only that. Our sex difference is a *climactic moment* in God's grand finale where creational differences are singing together in harmony. Here's how New Testament scholar N.T. Wright puts it:

> [T]he coming together of male plus female is itself a signpost pointing to that great complementarity of God's whole creation, of heaven and earth belonging together.[2]

Sex difference is not some fringe idea tacked onto the passage like some unrelated appendage. It's woven into the very fabric of God's good creation. Male and female, like the rest of creation, is singing together in harmony. Unity among difference. Now, marriage might be implied in Genesis 1 in God's command to "be fruitful and multiply" (Gen 1:28). But it's not explicitly mentioned until Genesis 2.

Genesis 2 is like a closer, more intimate look at day 6, the creation of humanity. And it's here in Genesis 2 where sex differences are explored and celebrated even more explicitly. For instance, Genesis 2:18 and 20 describes Eve as a "*suitable* helper" for Adam. It's tough to pick up in English, but the Hebrew word for "suitable" (*kenegdo*) expresses both sameness and difference. *Kenegdo* is a combination of two Hebrew words: *ki* which means *as*, *like*, or *similar*, and *neged*, which means something like *opposite* or *against*. The combination of both words (*ki* + *neged* = *kenegdo*) captures Eve's similarity to Adam and her difference.

So, Eve is similar to Adam since she's *human* and she's different from Adam since she's _____.

And however you fill in that blank will have important theological implications. I don't think it's much of a stretch to say that the difference Eve brings to the table is her *sex* difference—her *femaleness*.

A few verses later, Adam and Eve come together in marriage. As you read this passage, I want you to be on the lookout for the same stuff expressed in *kenegdo* above; that is, similarity and difference.

> Then the man said, "This at last is bone of my bone, and flesh of my flesh; she shall be called Woman, because she was taken out of Man." (Gen 2:23 ESV)
>
> *Therefore* a man shall leave his father and his mother and hold fast to his wife, and they shall become one flesh. (Gen 2:24 ESV)

As most everyone knows, Genesis 2:24 is the "John 3:16" of all marriage passages. It's often quoted throughout the New Testament (and in Judaism around the same time) to express the essential nature of what marriage is. What people often miss is the word "therefore" at the beginning of the verse. Whenever you see the word "therefore" in the Bible, you need to ask: "What's that *therefore* there *for*?" That is, what's the logical connection between Genesis 2:23 and 2:24?

The connection has to do with similarity and difference, the stuff expressed earlier in *kenegdo*. Adam's statement "bone of my bone, and flesh of my flesh" recognizes Eve's similarity. Eve is *like Adam* since she's human. And then he says: "She shall be called Woman, because she was taken out of Man." This is a statement about difference—sex difference, to be precise.

Here's the point, and it's a super important theological point: *The word* therefore *takes the common humanity and sex difference of Genesis 2:23 and bakes it into the very meaning of marriage expressed in Genesis 2:24.* The two that become "one flesh" in 2:24 are not just two consensual humans; they are precisely two sexually different humans.

So, according to Genesis chapters 1 and 2, sex-difference is not an if-you-feel-like-it option for marriage. It's an essential part of what marriage *is*.

And Jesus confirms this in Matthew 19. Look at how he quotes Genesis 2:24 in such a way that emphasizes sex difference *even more* than its original context:

> At the beginning the Creator "made them male and female" [quoting Gen 1:27] and said, "*Therefore* a man will leave his father and mother and be united to his wife, and the two will become one flesh?" (Matt 19:4–6, quoting Gen 2:24)

Notice that Jesus quotes Genesis 2:24 but instead of connecting it to Genesis 2:23, he brings in Genesis 1:27— an even more explicit statement about sex difference: "The Creator 'made them *male* and *female*'." According to Jesus' logic, the word *therefore* grabs hold of male and female sex difference in Genesis 1:27 and builds it into the definition of marriage in Genesis 2:24. Just like its original context in Genesis 2, "the two" who "will become one flesh" are precisely the "male and female" cited in Genesis 1:27.

The one-flesh marriage union Jesus speaks of is not simply two consensual humans; it's precisely the union between two sexually different persons.

In summary, Christianity hasn't just traditionally *assumed* that marriage is between a man and a woman—we need to be *biblicists*, not just *traditionalists*. Rather, the Bible says that sex-difference is necessary for what marriage is in the first place. There's nothing in the Bible or in Christian tradition that says marriage is a genderless institution.

## What about Eddy's Divorce?

Okay, so what about Eddy's divorce? Does the fact that we accept him mean that we should accept same-sex marriage?

No, I don't think it does. It's true that some Christians (certainly not all) have ignored the widespread problem of divorce and remarriage. There's no excuse for this. We should acknowledge it. Own it. And repent from it. In fact, I would go so far to say that one of the blessings of the LGBT+ conversation is that it has forced the church to reflect on its own sins and ask: *How can we be more holy in our marital and sexual lives?* Pornography, sexual lust, sex outside of marriage, and yes—unbiblical divorce. Straight Christians need to own it all. When it comes to sexual sins, we *all* fall short of God's standard.

That said, there's no logical or ethical or biblical reason why laxity in one area (divorce) should encourage laxity in another (same-sex marriage). I can't imagine Jesus looking at the church's divorce rate and saying, "Well, since you all have really dropped the ball by divorcing your spouses, I think it's only fair that you stop believing what I said about sex difference in marriage."

We should acknowledge that not every divorce is against God's will. Jesus allows for divorce if there's been sexual infidelity (Matt 5), and Paul says that if an unbelieving spouse leaves, the believing spouse is no longer bound to that marriage (1 Cor 7). While divorce isn't encouraged, the Bible does make some allowances. But the same is simply not true of same-sex marriage. The Bible never gives the slightest hint that sex-difference is somehow irrelevant or optional for marriage. Sex-difference is fundamental to what marriage is.

Let's revisit our opening dialogue and see what this could look like:

> Kristy asks, "Then why did your Uncle Eddy get divorced and remarried? Does the Bible say that divorce is fine?"
>
> "No," you say, "the Bible doesn't say that divorce is fine, but it does make some allowances for

divorce. It never says that same-sex marriages are sometimes okay."

"Even so," Kristy says, "the church is super tolerant on divorce and straight people committing all kinds of sexual sins, but it's utterly intolerant toward gay people. Sure feels like hypocrisy."

"You know what?" you say. "You're right."

"I'm what?"

"You're right. And I'm so sorry for this. The church *has* been hypocritical. *I've* been hypocritical. We *have* been intolerant toward gay people and much more lenient on divorce, adultery, greed, promiscuity, and all kinds of other sins. And looking back at Eddy's remarriage, I don't know. Maybe you're right. Maybe I shouldn't have gone to the wedding. I'm sorry for the inconsistencies in my life."

"So ... you think it's fine for me to marry Megan then?"

"Well, no. Just because we've been lenient toward some sins doesn't mean we should redefine marriage. Think about it another way. The church has not always done a good job helping the poor.

But that doesn't mean we should therefore be lenient toward racism also. What we need to do is help the poor *and* confront racism. Same with marriage. We should hold *all* people to a high standard, a biblical standard, for marriage. And again, I'm terribly sorry that we've been inconsistent and turned a blind eye to things like divorce."

Notice something about this version of the dialogue. You didn't get all defensive about Eddy's divorce. You were willing to admit that the church *has* been hypocritical and that they made a mistake. Admitting this doesn't mean you're endorsing same-sex marriage. It just means you're being honest and humble. After all, it's much easier to vilify the sins you don't struggle with.

When you're in conversations such as this, admitting you've been wrong and repenting from hypocrisy, inconsistency, and sins in your own life—or sins committed by others in the church—will go a long way toward sustaining an authentic relationship with that person. And relationships are the best context for truth to flourish.

> For a thorough discussion of the wedding question, see pastoral paper: "Should Christians Attend a Same-Sex Wedding Ceremony?"

## Should You Attend Kristy's Wedding?

So, does this mean you should attend Kristy's wedding?

The whole "Should I Attend a Same-Sex Wedding?" question is a tough one! And I don't think there's one crystal-clear response that every Christian must give. There is no verse or passage in the Bible that says you should or shouldn't attend a same-sex wedding. Whether you attend is a gray area similar to the "disputable matters" Paul talks about in Romans 14. Put simply, we're not talking about a sin-versus-not-sin decision. It's more of a wise-versus-unwise decision that must take into account the specific relationships of the people involved. For some, attending may be the wiser thing to do, while for others it may be unwise to attend. It's all part of the *grace/truth* tension. Those who don't attend are trying to give allegiance to the truth, yet they may sever a relationship with the person getting married. Those who attend are trying to maintain a relationship with the person, yet they may give the impression that they agree with same-sex marriages.

With that in mind, here are four different responses (though not the only ones) that I believe can be a faithful Christian response. Again, there's no chapter or verse that gives us a black-and-white "right" answer. Think through each of the following and wrestle with which one you think is the best *grace/truth* response:

**Response 1: Attend.** "Kristy, I'm honored that you invited me to your wedding. I love you and want to support you, and I don't want to do anything that might hinder our relationship. I may not agree with same-sex marriage, but I can still attend and support you in your decision because you are my friend and I know this means so much to you."

Some Christians may balk at this response. They believe you should only attend weddings that are in line with Scripture. And I can respect that. I would, however, encourage you to make sure that if you choose *not* to attend a same-sex wedding, you also refrain from attending *any* wedding that conflicts with Scripture, such as a wedding where one of the partners has gone through an unbiblical divorce, or a wedding between a confessing Christian and a non-Christian. In any case, those who choose to attend a same-sex wedding are prioritizing the relationship between themselves and their loved one who is getting married. They may not agree with the marriage itself, but their attendance is an expression of love and commitment to the *person*, even if they don't agree with the morality of the marriage itself.

**Response 2: Ask for time to think.** "Kristy, I love you so much, and despite what you may think, I truly do want you to be happy and live a fulfilling life. But I really need some time to process this. Can you respect that? I'm truly trying to live by my convictions, as any person should, but I'm also trying to love you the best way that I know how. I would actually love to meet your fiancée, Megan. I may not agree with same-sex marriage, but I want to love the person whom you love."

This isn't a yes-or-no response, and yet it conveys your heart in wanting to honor Kristy while staying true to your convictions. The beauty of this response is that whether you end up deciding yes or no, Kristy will know that you at least took time to consider it and weren't responding out of a knee-jerk reaction to your views on homosexuality.

**Response 3: Attend the reception but not the wedding.** "Kristy, I'm honored that you'd ask me to attend your wedding. I love you and want to be there for you, but you know what I believe about marriage, and I feel that I would dishonor my beliefs if I attend. But I still want to be there for you and show you that I care. Would it be okay if I attend your reception instead of your ceremony? A reception isn't the same as the ceremony, and I feel that I can be a part of that without going against my convictions."

This response prioritizes the sanctity of the wedding ceremony while also trying to prioritize the sanctity of your relationship with Kristy. It's an attempt to show your love for Kristy while staying true to your convictions about the wedding ceremony. This response may go well with Kristy, or it could backfire and be interpreted as an attempt to throw Kristy some scraps of food while saying, "Be warm and filled" (James 2 ESV). Be sure to think through the specific relationship you have with your LGBT+ loved one before you give this response.

**Response 4: Don't attend.** "Kristy, you know I love you and I consider you a friend. But you also know my convictions about same-sex marriage. I simply can't attend your wedding, since it would violate my conscience and my ethical beliefs. While I love you and still want to be friends, I can't show support for something that I don't agree with."

I respect those who would never attend a same-sex wedding. They are seeking to stay true to what God says about marriage and don't want to give any impression that they are bending on the truth. Most often, not attending a wedding ceremony of a loved one (especially a child or sibling) will sever or significantly impair the relationship, so you have to consider the likely fallout. At the same time, it's not good for a Christian to violate their conscience, so if attending a same-sex wedding does, then it may not be good to attend.

There are other responses you could give (see the pastoral paper in the sidebar where I give seven different responses). The important thing is to not try to make this decision on your own. I'd highly recommend talking it through with your Christian leaders and other godly people you trust, preferably those who understand the *grace/truth* tension of the question.

One last word of advice to parents with an LGBT+ son or daughter, or anyone who has an LGBT+ person who is very close to them. Wherever you land on the attend-or-not-attend question, it's incredibly important that you show love and value toward your loved one's partner. I've heard a lot of gay kids in this situation say, *The best way for my parents to show me love is to love the person that I love, even if they disagree with my marriage.* And again, if Jesus is the perfect embodiment of truth *and* grace, as we saw in conversation 2, then Christians should be quite eager to show love toward any person, even—or especially—if they fall short of God's ethical standard.

## QUESTIONS FOR DISCUSSION

1. What questions or arguments raised by Kristy were initially most persuasive to you, and how would you respond?

2. Can you think of a "Thou shall not marry a person of the same sex" verse in Scripture? Or which verses do you think would be relevant for addressing same-sex marriage?

3. I've suggested four possible responses above to the question: *Should you attend Kristy's wedding?* Which one would you choose and why? Or, is there another response you would give?

4. My friend Bill encourages Christians to attend a same-sex wedding of a friend or relative. He says, "Being 'right' for one day [that is, *not* attending] can damage the opportunity to be a witness for thousands of days into the future. Think long term." What do you think about this advice?

5. Regarding the "attend a same-sex wedding" question, do you think it should make a difference if the couple getting married claims to be Christian? Why or why not.

6. Do you believe that the Bible defines marriage as a union between a man and a woman? Have you heard any compelling biblical arguments from affirming Christians that marriage is a genderless institution?

7. How is your thinking challenged by the discussion above of the biblical statements about sex-difference in marriage? Without even looking at prohibitions about gay sex, do you believe these biblical passages rule out same-sex marriage in the church?

8. Some Christians say they oppose same-sex marriage *in the church*, but don't oppose it for *society as a whole*. That is, they're fine with the Supreme Court decision in June 2015 that legalized same-sex marriage, and yet they still believe that churches should stay true to the fact that the Bible defines marriage as between one man and one woman. Do you agree or disagree with this? Why?

9. Do you think that the church has been hypocritical toward gay people and same-sex marriages while it has been soft on other sins (unbiblical divorces, pornography, etc.) committed by heterosexual Christians? Why or why not?

10. What do you think of offering to have lunch with Kristy and her partner to get to know her partner better? Is this a "slippery slope" or an expression of Christian love?

## CHAPTER ENDNOTES

**1** For example, see Colby Martin, *Unclobber: Rethinking our Misuse of the Bible on Homosexuality* (Louisville: Westminster John Knox, 2016).

**2** N. T. Wright, "What Is Marriage For? Tracing God's Plan from Genesis to Revelation," *Plough Quarterly*, September 2015. www.plough.com/en/topics/life/marriage/what-is-marriage-for

# What Does the Bible Say about Same-Sex Sexual Relations?

Welcome back to our study! I want to alert you up front that this conversation will probably be the most intellectually intense conversation of our study. For those of you who are analytical—the engineers and math teachers among us—you'll probably love this conversation the most. If you're more relationally driven, this conversation might require more digesting. But both are important: relationships and intellect. Jesus said we should love God with all our heart *and our minds* (Matt 22:37), and Paul said we should be transformed by the renewing of our mind (Rom 12:1–2). Yet even as we strap on our thinking caps and wrestle with some passages, we must never lose sight of the fact that we're talking about *people*.

In this conversation, we're going to look at the passages that directly mention some sort of same-sex sexual behavior. There are six such passages: three in the Old Testament (Gen 19:1–10; Lev 18:22; 20:13) and three in the New (Rom 1:26–27; 1 Cor 6:9; 1 Tim 1:9–10). As you're looking at these passages, you may wonder: *How can affirming Christians read these passages and say that same-sex sexual relations are morally permissible?* Most affirming Christians must find a way to interpret these passages so that they don't apply to same-sex monogamous marital relations.

Please note: The debate is not over what the Bible *says*. With a gazillion English translations just a Google away, everyone knows what the relevant verses *say*. The debate is over what these verses *mean*. This distinction is so important! Whenever Christians debate this topic, it's inevitable that the traditional side will bring up one of these verses. "Well, you know, Fred, Romans 1 says … " and he goes on to quote Romans 1, as if Fred (the affirming one, if you didn't notice) doesn't know what Romans 1 *says*. He knows what it says. But Fred probably feels that conservative Christians have wrongly understood what these verses *mean*.

We need to go beyond simple *observation* (what the Bible *says*) and do the tough work of *interpretation* (what the Bible *means*).

So we're going to go through each of the six prohibition passages and spend most of our time addressing the reasons affirming Christians say these verses don't apply to modern-day same-sex marriages.

## The Laws of Leviticus

There are two laws in Leviticus that condemn male same-sex sexual behavior: Leviticus 18:22 and 20:13:

> "Do not have sexual relations with a man as one does with a woman; that is detestable."
> (Lev 18:22 NIV)

> "If a man has sexual relations with a man as one does with a woman, both of them have done what is detestable. They are to be put to death; their blood will be on their own heads." (Lev 20:13 NIV)

Both verses say it's wrong for a man to have sex with another man. This seems pretty clear, and biblical scholars agree that this is what the verse says.[1] So, how do affirming Christians interpret these Levitical prohibitions? (Remember: we're wrestling with what these verses *mean*, not just what they *say*.) Here are two popular responses.

## 1. Old Testament laws are no longer binding on Christians

Some say that since these commands are in Leviticus and part of Old Testament law, Christians don't need to obey them because they are no longer under the law. Sure, it was wrong for *Israel* to engage in same-sex behavior. But it was also wrong for Israel to eat pork, trim their beards, and gather sticks on Saturday. Christians, however, aren't under these laws. They were for *Israel*.

While this argument can still be seen in blogs and pop-theology books, most thoughtful affirming Christians don't use it any more. It's not a very good argument, and here's why. *Just because some Old Testament laws are obsolete doesn't mean all laws are.* There are many Old Testament laws that are still binding on Christians, including several laws right here in Leviticus 18–20: Incest (vv. 18:6–18; 20:11–14, 17, 19–21), adultery (vv. 18:20; 20:10), child sacrifice (vv. 18:21; 20:1–5), bestiality (vv. 18:23; 20:15–16), theft (v. 19:11), lying (v. 19:11), taking the Lord's name in vain (v. 19:20), oppressing your neighbor (v. 19:13), and many others—all in the same context as the same-sex laws. It's in Leviticus, in fact, that we get the central Christian command to "love your neighbor as yourself" (Lev 19:18).

Just because *some* laws are obsolete doesn't mean all laws are. Lots of Levitical laws are still binding on Christians.

In fact, if you read Leviticus 18 you'll see that this chapter deals almost exclusively with sexual immorality, and all the laws about sexual immorality are carried over into the New Testament—including the prohibitions about same-sex sexual behavior.[2] There's no convincing reason Leviticus 18:22 and 20:13 should not be applicable for Christians while laws about adultery, incest, and bestiality *are* applicable.[3]

## 2. Same-sex prohibitions address nonconsensual sex

Another argument affirming Christians make is that consensual, monogamous, same-sex relations didn't exist in the ancient world. Sure, it was common for masters to have sex with their male slaves, older men to have sex with younger teenage boys, or victims of war to be raped by their male conquerors. But these are acts of *sexual exploitation*, not consensual love.

So, do the prohibitions in Leviticus refer only to *exploitative* same-sex acts (e.g., a master raping his male slave)? Or do they include *consensual* same-sex acts as well?

Of course exploitative acts are forbidden. The Bible would never sanction a master raping his slave, or any other act of sexual violence (see Deut 22:25–27). But there's nothing in Leviticus 18:22 and 20:13 that *limits* the prohibition to acts of sexual exploitation. Again, don't just believe me. Go back and carefully read the prohibitions. Do they mention masters or slaves or prostitutes or rape or older men having sex with teenage boys? The language of Leviticus simply says that men (not just masters, or older men, or victors of war) shouldn't lie sexually with another male (not just slaves, or younger boys, or war victims). There's nothing in the text or around the text that limits the prohibition to acts of exploitation. In fact, Leviticus 20:13 (NIV) says that if a man has sex with another male, "*both of them* have done what is detestable." Clearly the act was mutual.

Some affirming Christians say that the biblical text doesn't need to specifically mention exploitation since *every same-sex relationship in the ancient world was exploitative*. But this simply isn't true either. For what it's worth, we know very little about the sexual practices of same-sex relations in the ancient world. But the evidence we do have is somewhat diverse. We have evidence of exploitative same-sex relations,

> For a thorough discussion about consensual same-sex relations in the biblical world, see the pastoral paper "Did Consensual Same-Sex Relations Exist in the Biblical World?"

but we also have evidence of consensual relations.[4]
We can't just assume that all same-sex acts back then
were abusive. Most apparently were, but some weren't.
And Leviticus doesn't limit its same-sex prohibitions to
abusive acts. All types of male same-sex behavior are
condemned.

In short, if you *look at the text* and *study its historical
context*, there's no evidence that Leviticus was
prohibiting only certain types of same-sex behavior.

## The Sin of Sodom

Before we leave the Old Testament, we need to mention
the story of Sodom (Gen 19:1–10). As you may recall, a
couple of angels show up at Lot's house, and the men of
Sodom mistake the angels for men. After trying to gang
rape the two angels, the men of the city are struck with
blindness as divine punishment for their evil attempt.

Many evangelical theologians point out that what's
happening in Genesis 19 is *not* consensual same-
sex love; it's *attempted sexual violence*. It's like an
ancient version of modern-day prison rape. If a man in
prison rapes another man, it's usually not because the
perpetrator was gay. It's an act of domination and power.
Likewise, the men of Sodom were trying to gang rape

Lot's guests. They weren't courting Lot's guests, bringing them flowers and asking them out for a romantic stroll under the desert moonlight. They were trying to gang rape them.

Now here's the thing: Most scholars who interpret the passage this way hold to a historically Christian view of marriage. They're obviously not trying to bend Scripture around their view. They're just trying to be honest interpreters of the Bible.

Put simply: I don't think the story of Sodom (Gen 19) is a very relevant passage for understanding what God thinks about modern-day, consensual same-sex relations.

For a thorough discussion about the story of Sodom, see the pastoral paper "Was the 'Sin of Sodom' Homosexuality?"

Now it's true that *if* the men of Sodom had gone ahead and raped the two men (or angels), they still would have violated Leviticus 18:22 and 20:13. But it's important to stay focused on the main point and the main sin. Consensual same-sex love is nowhere to be found in Genesis 19, and yet consensual same-sex love is the pressing ethical question facing the church. To use the Sodom story as evidence that God prohibits consensual same-sex sexual relationships is probably not the best use of this text.

In fact, whenever the Bible talks about the "sin of Sodom," it never mentions homosexuality.[5] The Bible usually describes Sodom as a city that was greedy and prideful. Check out Ezekiel:

> Now this was the sin of your sister Sodom: She and her daughters were arrogant, overfed and unconcerned; they did not help the poor and needy. They were haughty and did detestable things before me (16:49–50 NIV).

Wow! Did you get that? Ezekiel says that the real sin of Sodom was that it was overfed, arrogant, and unconcerned for the poor. It's pretty sad when overfed, greedy Christians who perfectly fit Ezekiel's description run around hating on gay people. In fact, the Bible gives a different picture of who the real "Sodomites" are. Many of them are overstuffed, materialistic straight people.

So in the end, the story of Sodom tells us that attempted gang rape is wrong, but it doesn't tell us much about loving, consensual same-sex relations.

## New Testament Prohibitions

Three passages in the New Testament prohibit same-sex behavior. The most important is Romans 1:

> For this reason God gave them up to dishonorable passions. For their women exchanged natural relations for those that are contrary to nature; and the men likewise gave up natural relations with women and were consumed with passion for one another, men committing shameless acts with men and receiving in themselves the due penalty for their error (Rom 1:26–27 ESV).

The other two times same-sex sexual behavior is mentioned is in 1 Corinthians and 1 Timothy (both passages are the author's translation):[6]

> Or do you not know that the unrighteous will not inherit the kingdom of God? Do not be deceived: neither the sexually immoral, nor idolaters, nor adulterers, *nor men who have sex with males*, nor thieves, nor the greedy, nor drunkards, nor revilers, nor swindlers will inherit the kingdom of God (1 Cor 6:9–10).

> Understanding this, that the law is not laid down for the just but for the lawless and disobedient, for the ungodly and sinners, for the unholy and profane, for those who strike their fathers and mothers, for murderers, the sexually immoral, *men who have sex with males*, enslavers, liars, perjurers,

and whatever else is contrary to sound doctrine
(1 Tim 1:9–10).

These passages seem rather clear. So how do affirming
Christians interpret them? Again, it's important to make
sure we actually listen to and try to understand these
arguments. Listening doesn't mean *agreeing*. But you
can't disagree until you understand what it is you're
disagreeing with.

With that in mind, here are three popular affirming
responses.

## 1. All the New Testament prohibitions refer to nonconsensual sex

One of the most popular affirming interpretations
for these New Testament passages is the same
"nonconsensual" argument we saw above in reference
to the Old Testament passages. Again, some say that
the only type of same-sex relations that existed in the
ancient world—including the Greco-Roman world of the
New Testament—were exploitative. Rape, prostitution,
and pederasty (i.e., older men having sexual relations
with teenage boys).

Our two-fold response to this argument is same one we
gave above. *Look at the text* and *study its context*.

As with the Leviticus passages, there's nothing in these New Testament passages that mentions masters or slaves or prostitutes or rape or older men having sex with boys (pederasty). In fact, there are several different Greek words for pederasty, and none of them are used in these passages.[7] None of them actually occur in the New Testament. The biblical writers would have condemned pederasty, but they didn't *only* condemn pederasty. All types of male-male sexual relations were considered to be outside of God's will and design.

What's fascinating is that several *affirming* scholars actually agree with this point. For instance, the late Louis Crompton, a self-identified gay man and a brilliant scholar who wrote a highly acclaimed book called *Homosexuality and Civilization*, says:

> Nowhere does Paul or any other Jewish writer of this period imply the least acceptance of same-sex relations under any circumstance. The idea that homosexuals might be redeemed by mutual devotion would have been wholly foreign to Paul or any other Jew or early Christian.[8]

Bill Loader is the world's foremost scholar on sexuality in ancient Christianity and Judaism. And he's an affirming Christian. Still, *he rejects the argument that the only same-sex relationships in the ancient world were exploitative.* Loader says that Paul's words in Romans 1:26–27 "included, but [were] by no means limited to exploitative pederasty," "sexual abuse of male slaves," or "same-sex acts … performed within idolatrous ritual contexts."[9] And again: "It is inconceivable that [Paul] would approve of any same-sex acts if, as we must assume, he affirmed the prohibitions of Leviticus 18:22 and 20:13 as fellow Jews of his time understood them."[10]

The idea that New Testament writers were prohibiting *only* exploitative same-sex relations is neither biblically nor historically accurate.

An offshoot of this argument focuses specifically on idolatrous same-sex sexual behavior. That is, some affirming Christians say that Paul has in mind cultic male prostitution or other same-sex acts associated with Greco-Roman paganism.

It's true that Romans 1 is all about idolatry. Just before Paul mentions same-sex behavior in verses 1:26–27, he talks about people who "exchanged the glory of the immortal God for images made to look like a mortal human being and birds and animals and reptiles" (1:23). The problem with this argument, however, is that it misunderstands what Paul means by idolatry. Paul doesn't say that same-sex behavior associated with pagan idolatry is wrong while non-idolatrous same-sex acts are right. Rather, he says that *all sin* is idolatry—a turning away from the Creator's design and turning in on itself for glory and satisfaction. Just as Ezekiel talked about "idols of the heart" (Ezek 14), Paul says that a heart turned away from its Creator is an idolatrous heart. This includes *all* the sins in Romans 1, not just the same-sex sins: sexual impurity, greed, envy, murder, strife, deceit, malice, gossip, and on and on Paul goes (esp. 1:29–31). It's *all* idolatry—some of which you and I undoubtedly committed this morning! Because a heart turned away from God's design for human flourishing is an idolatrous heart.

## 2. Paul is condemning straight people having gay sex, which is against "their nature"

This argument is based on Romans 1:26, where Paul says, "For their women exchanged natural relations for those that are *contrary to nature*." Some affirming Christians argue that God is only condemning heterosexuals who have abandoned their *natural desire for* the opposite sex and instead pursue sexual relations with people of the same sex. In other words, the "nature" Paul is referring to is their natural sexual orientation. Straight people shouldn't have gay sex.

This interpretation, however, doesn't follow what Paul is actually saying. He does not say "contrary to *their* nature," but "contrary to nature" (the Greek *para physin*). Paul is not saying some people left behind their innate heterosexual urges to pursue same-sex partners for whom they felt no innate desire. Rather, he's saying that some people have gone against the Creator's design (opposite sex relations) to pursue sexual relations with members of their same sex.

In fact, the phrase "contrary to nature" was often used by ancient philosophers and moral teachers who believed that same-sex sexual relations were wrong. They didn't think such acts were wrong simply *because* they went against one's own personal sexual orientation. Rather, these writers—including Paul—believed they were wrong because same-sex sexual relations go against the way humans have been designed, even if some people experience sexual desires for the same sex.

In short, Paul's phrase "contrary to nature" essentially means "contrary to God's intent for sexual expression."

## 3. The real problem in Romans 1 was excessive lust

A similar affirming argument says that the reason same-sex relations were condemned is because Paul considered them to be the result of excessive lust. That is, straight men got bored with having sex with women and, out of their lust, explored new and kinky territory with other men.

So, the previous argument focuses on the *types* of same-sex relations. This argument focuses on the *reasons* men were having sex with other males. Both arguments are trying to create a distinction between the same-sex relations back then and the same-sex relations today.

For a thorough discussion of these and other affirming arguments, see the pastoral paper "15 Reasons Why Some Christians Affirm Same-Sex Relations: And 15 Responses."

If you look at Romans 1, you can see where this argument comes from. Paul says that men "were consumed with passion for one another" (Rom 1:27), which sure sounds like lust. But pay close attention to what Paul is writing. Is lust the *reason* these relations were wrong?

No. If you look at the broader context, Paul's point is that men departed from their Creator's design by having sex with other males. Of course there's passion and desire involved. That kind of goes hand in hand with any sex act—gay or straight! (Could any couple have sex and *not* be "consumed with passion for one another?") But the passion or lust is not the *reason* Paul says gay sex is wrong. Crossing God-designed gender boundaries is.

// // //

I want to stress again that the biblical teaching about same-sex marriage doesn't depend on these five or six passages alone. They simply confirm what we saw in our previous conversation: that sex-difference is a necessary part of what marraige is and that all sexual relationships outside of marriage are sin. The prohibition passages are simply a few of many passages that prohibit sex outside of marriage (properly defined).

Now just to be clear, the arguments discussed above are only *some* of the affirming arguments that have to do with the prohibition passages. In *Grace/Truth 2.0*, we interact with many other affirming arguments, such as:

- Aren't LGBT+ people "born that way?" And if so, isn't it immoral not let them express their sexuality according to how God created them to be?

- Doesn't the Bible give an ethical trajectory toward accepting same-sex marriages?

- The Bible is super patriarchal; therefore, can it be trusted to teach us about marriage in the twenty-first century?

- Shouldn't Christians just love everyone?

- Haven't Christians been on the wrong side of history before?

- Since Jesus never mentions homosexuality, why do Christians make a big deal about it?

- Is this a "disputable matter," like the nature of baptism or drinking alcohol?

Or if you don't want to wait until *Grace/Truth 2.0*, you can find a response to these (and other) affirming arguments in our pastoral paper "15 Reasons Why Some Christians Affirm Same-Sex Relations: And 15 Responses," referenced above.

## People before Arguments

Now here's the thing that may frustrate some of you (especially the analytically minded) and refresh others of you (the relationally driven). People are rarely convinced of something by logical arguments alone, as renowned psychologist Jonathan Haidt has recently shown.[11] If you show no love, no concern, no compassion, no empathy, no willingness to understand another person's point of view, you will rarely, if ever, convince them of the truth. Your

The greatest apologetic for truth—is love.

attitude carries more power than your arguments. Try to remember this next time you find yourself in a discussion (or debate) with someone about LGBT+ related questions. We should never lose sight of the stuff we talked about in conversation 2, *"Grace/Truth—the Jesus Way,"* when we're reaching for our biblical artillery to win an argument. Sure, you may win the argument, but you'll probably lose the person.

The fact is, our truth will not be heard until our grace is felt. Because the greatest apologetic for truth—is love.

1. Do you believe that the laws of Leviticus 18:22 and 20:13 are binding on Christians (as discussed above)? Why or why not.

2. Read through the sexual laws in Leviticus 18:6–23. Do you see any that might not apply to Christians? Why or why not? (Some people say that 18:19 doesn't apply. See endnote 2 for my response.)

3. Do you agree that the men of Sodom were probably not gay and that the story itself does not directly apply to modern-day, same-sex marriages? Why or why not?

4. If it's true that the sin of Sodom was not "being gay," why do you think many Christians believe it was?

5. Can you think of other affirming arguments that weren't mentioned in this conversation? (Again, we'll engage with several others in *Grace/Truth 2.0*.) Share those arguments.

6. Are there any other New Testament passages that you feel are relevant for this conversation, even if they don't directly address same-sex sexual relations? What are they?

7. Do you agree or disagree with this statement: "People are rarely convinced of something by logical arguments alone"? Have you experienced this in your own life, either when you were trying to convince someone else, or when someone was trying to convince you? Please discuss.

8. Some Christian leaders and scholars are changing their view of same-sex relations from historically Christian to affirming (e.g., Tony Campolo, David Gushee, Jen Hatmaker). Why do you think they are changing their view?

9. Do you have any questions or disagreements about the responses to the affirming arguments discussed in this conversation? Please discuss.

10. Can you think of a time when you changed your view on some sin because it happened in your life or in your family? (Divorce, remarriage, an addiction, etc.)

## CHAPTER ENDNOTES

**1** Female same-sex relations aren't mentioned in this text or anywhere in the Old Testament. The only place they are mentioned is in Rom 1:26. Female same-sex relations are rarely (perhaps never) mentioned outside the Old Testament during this time either. The first clear reference we have of lesbian relations comes in the writings of the poet Sappho (ca. 630–570 BC). So the Old Testament is not alone in its silence about female homoeroticism. Perhaps romantic love between women didn't exist in the Old Testament world, or, more likely, it was kept secret. Either way, it would be unnecessary for Leviticus to prohibit something that wasn't a visible issue needing to be addressed.

**2** The only possible exception is Lev 18:19, which says that a man shouldn't have sex with his wife while she is menstruating. Some people say that this law is no longer binding, but I've never actually seen a good argument that shows why it's totally okay for a husband to have sex while his wife is menstruating. There's nothing in the Bible that tells Christians that after Jesus' resurrection, they can go ahead and make love to their wives while they're menstruating.

**3** In fact, Paul describes and prohibits homosexual behavior by using a Greek word, *arsenokoites* (1 Cor 6:9; 1 Tim 1:9) that appears to have been created directly from the Greek translation of Lev 20:13. Therefore, we have evidence from the New Testament that the same-sex laws of Leviticus were still binding on Christians.

**4** Some examples of consensual same-sex relations in the Old Testament world can be found in the writings of Sappho (see endnote 1 above), in the wall paintings of the tomb of two Egyptian manicurists Niankhkhnum and Khnumhotep, which depicted the male couple as lovers, and in the nightly—and most probably sexual—visits that the Egyptian King Neferkare made to the home of his military commander Sasenet (around 1700 BC). For details, see Preston Sprinkle, "Same-Sex Relations," in *Dictionary of Daily Life in Biblical and Postbiblical Antiquity*, eds. Edwin Yamauchi and Marvin Wilson, vol. 4 (Peabody, MA: Hendrickson, 2017).

**5** See Isa 1:10–17; 3:9; Jer 23:14; Matt 10:5–10. Some think that Jude 7, which mentions the men of Sodom going after "strange flesh" (*sarkos heteras*), supports the traditional interpretation. But in the context, "strange flesh" refers not to people of the same sex but to angels—the ones whom the Sodomites were seeking to rape. The phrase "strange flesh" actually means "*other* flesh" and ironically contains the Greek word *heteras* from which we get *hetero*sexual. If *homo*sexual relations were what Jude had in mind, it would have made much more sense for him to say "same flesh" not "other flesh."

**6** As I argue elsewhere, the Greek terms *arsenokoites* and *malakoi* are best translated "men who have sex with males." I use "males" here instead of "men" as some translations have it (e.g., NIV), since "men" would limit the action to adults, while Paul's word includes males of all ages (see Sprinkle, *People to Be Loved*, 108–117)

**7** The Greek word *paiderastes* was widely used to refer to "the love of boys," as was *paidophthoros* ("corruptor of boys") or *paidophtoreo* ("seducer of boys"). Another pair of Greek words, *erastes* and *eromenos*, were often used to describe the older man (*erastes*) and his boy-lover (*eromenos*). Again, none of these words are used when the New Testament prohibits same-sex relations.

**8** Louis Crompton, *Homosexuality and Civilization* (Cambridge, MA: Belknap Press, 2006), 114.

**9** William Loader, *The New Testament on Sexuality, Attitudes Towards Sexuality in Judaism and Christianity in the Hellenistic Greco-Roman Era* (Grand Rapids: Eerdmans, 2012), 325.

**10** Ibid., 322.

**11** See Jonathan Haidt, *The Righteous Mind: Why Good People Are Divided by Politics and Religion* (New York: Vintage Press, 2013).

# Six Relational Do's and Don'ts

The last conversation was a bit heavy and intellectually driven. This final conversation will be almost exclusively relational. Whenever I dive deep into a topic, I always need to know, "How do I live this stuff out? What does this look like 'on the ground'?" That's what we're going to explore in this conversation. We're going to look at six different relational practices that capture the *grace/ truth* way.

## 1. Listen, Learn, and Listen Again

The number one thing I've learned in talking to LGBT+ people is the power of listening. To listen intently, to listen with an attitude of humility and openness, is an act of love, and you can't love without listening. This means that Christians should be the best listeners on the planet! Unfortunately, with this topic, we haven't been.

A few years ago, I made it a point to sit down and just listen to LGBT+ people. I wanted to hear their stories, feel their heart, get to know them authentically. I was disappointed at how many of them said, "I've never had a Christian tell me they just want to listen to me."

Some people say that we don't need to listen. We just need to speak truth into people's lives. Those same people may dish out the truth quite willingly, but they may be unable to receive the truth when someone speaks it into *their* lives. In any case, healthy relationships are built on trust, and people won't trust you if you won't even listen to them. Yes, we should speak truth into the lives of people—and receive truth into our own lives—but we won't be given this opportunity if we're not genuine listeners.

Listening is the bridge that forms and solidifies authentic relationships. And truth is best spoken and received in the context of relationships.

Let's apply this to a situation where a gay teenager comes out to his parents. If I've learned anything about this type of conversation it is this: the number-one thing parents should do in this situation is listen. Don't talk. Don't preach. Just listen, listen, and listen again.

Imagine that you are sixteen years old. You've experienced unwanted same-sex attractions for three years. You've stayed up late trying to "pray it away." You've risen early begging God to "fix you." You've cried. You've screamed. You've struggled alone—for three years. You've experienced crushing anxiety and debilitating depression. You've felt shame, confusion, doubt, anger, despair—and you've gone through all of this *alone*. For three years. With no one to talk to. You've contemplated suicide—maybe even attempted it. And finally, after many long, agonizing, lonely nights wrestling with yourself, you've decided to tell your parents. You're frightened beyond belief. *Will they reject me? Will they hate me? Will they accept me and walk with me in my journey?* Finally, the day has come, and you look your parents in the eye and tell them: "Mom ... Dad ... I think I'm ... gay."

> To listen intently, to listen with an attitude of humility and openness, is an act of love, and you can't love without listening. This means that Christians should be the best listeners on the planet!

How would you want them to respond?

Unfortunately, most LGBT+ people, who have come out to their parents, have experienced shame, shock, and dehumanizing rhetoric from their parents in this moment. And that horrific moment is forever etched into their memory and can never leave.

But what if your parents, with eyes full of compassion, stared into your soul, reaffirmed their unconditional love for you, and just listened? To listen is to love, and you can't love without listening. The number one thing you can do when your LGBT+ friend or relative comes out to you is to listen, listen, and listen again. When it is your turn to talk, the first words out of your mouth should be "I love you, and I'm committed to you no matter what. You are so special to me, and you are infinitely special to God. There's nothing I would love to do more right now than to listen to your story."

If you want more helpful information on how to be a loving parent or friend to an LGBT+ person who comes out to you, please see the incredibly helpful resource *Guiding Families of LGBT+ Loved Ones* (2nd edition) put out by Lead Them Home ministries (www.leadthem home.org/get-resources/guiding-families-lgbt-loved -ones). It's the single best resource I've ever seen on this topic.

## 2. Pay Close Attention to Your Language

By language, I'm not talking about dropping F-bombs and dirty jokes. I'm talking about using words and phrases correctly. Remember our opening conversation about the terms *gay, same-sex attraction*, and *LGBT+*? We saw how important it is to pay close attention to our words and phrases, including avoiding certain phrases that have caused a lot of pain in conversations such as this.

With that in mind, here are a few words and phrases we should avoid saying:

### The Gay Lifestyle

Too often, the terms *gay* or *homosexual* are quickly followed by the word *lifestyle*. My friend Jordan in the opening story is living a life of celibacy. His "lifestyle" is one of sexual purity. But because he's attracted to the same sex, some straight people assume he's living "the gay lifestyle" and having tons of gay sex and is gearing up to march in the next pride parade. But he's not.

The term *lifestyle* is quite odd, if you think about it. Does every gay person have the same *lifestyle*? How would you feel if someone asked you if you were living the "straight lifestyle" and then lumped you into a category with every other straight person who walks the planet?

Many prostitutes and popes, porn stars and pastors, are straight. Does this mean they're living the "straight lifestyle?" Are you? I think you'd be bothered by the very question, since you are a unique person, not some clone cut out of straightness.

## Practicing Homosexual

Similar to *gay lifestyle,* this phrase just sounds goofy when you think about it. Again, how would you respond if someone asked you, "So, are you a practicing heterosexual?" I think I'd chuckle and ask, "What, do you think I'm working on my heterosexuality like my golf swing?" What we really want to know is whether they are sexually active. But unless you're friends with the person, you probably don't have the right to know whether they are having sex. How would you feel if a stranger asked you about your sex life?

Let's drop this phrase from our vocabulary. It's like referring to African Americans as "colored folk." Not only is it out of date, but it's been used by so many unloving people over the years that it has taken on the scent of bigotry.

## Homosexual

I'd recommend never using the word *homosexual* when referring to people. Almost every gay person I know dislikes being called "a homosexual." It sounds impersonal, clinical, and outdated. It would be like walking into an IT department and asking for a floppy disk. There's nothing grammatically wrong with the phrase *floppy disk*. It just shows that you haven't cared enough about technology to keep up with the discussion. In the same way, *homosexual* is often used by straight people who don't know any gay people, or who haven't cared enough to keep up with the discussion.

Almost every gay person I know prefers to be called gay, lesbian, or queer.

## The Gay Agenda

Another broad-brush term. People sometimes use the phrase *the gay agenda* to refer to political activists who advocate for bathroom policies and LGBT+ sex education in schools. And let me be clear—all of this is alive and real. I don't deny that some people, gay and straight, do have an agenda. However, not every gay person has some unified agenda, which makes the phrase *the gay agenda* nonsensical.

If there's no universal straight agenda, or male agenda, or American agenda, then the same goes for the so-called gay agenda. Let's focus on people and drop the stereotypes.

## Love the Sinner, Hate the Sin

There's some truth to this phrase. We should love sinners and would should hate sin. But this phrase often has a condescending, self-righteous ring to it. The person saying it comes off as someone who has all their stuff together—after all, they are loving all those poor, lowly sinners while hating their sin. It feels judgmental, and it doesn't work in real relationships."Honey, you're such a sinner, but I love you anyway, you sinner. And I absolutely hate your sin." See how that goes over on your honeymoon!

Every LGBT+ person I know has heard this phrase spoken over them, and I don't know a single one who likes the phrase—even my LGBT+ friends who are born-again conservative Christians. They're always viewed as the sinner who has sin worthy of hate. Never mind the piles of sin committed by the one saying this phrase.

Instead of *love the sinner, hate the sin*, why not: Love the sinner, *hate your own sin*, and let's pursue Jesus together as broken people equally in need of grace?

Yeah, I like that last sentence a lot better. Let's coin it and make it our mantra in the LGBT+ conversation.

## 3. Gospel First, Sexuality Later

Have you ever been in a conversation with an LGBT+ person at work or in the community, and you wondered, *Do I need to tell this person where I stand on homosexuality?* I think it's important to understand that we weren't commissioned to preach a gospel of "Don't have gay sex" but rather "Believe on the Lord Jesus and you will be saved." To repeat an earlier point, the good news isn't "God can make you straight" but "God can make you holy." A message of sexual judgment detached from the gospel is legalism, not grace.

This is so important to keep in mind when interacting with all LGBT+ people, but especially people who are not yet Christian. Some Christians feel uneasy just talking to LGBT+ people. They feel that they *have* to tell them where they stand on questions related to sexuality and gender. But listen closely to Paul's words in 1 Corinthians 5:

> I wrote to you in my letter not to associate with sexually immoral people—not at all meaning the

> sexually immoral of this world, or the greedy and
> swindlers, or idolaters, since then you would need
> to go out of the world ... For what have I to do with
> judging outsiders? (1 Cor 5:9–10, 12 ESV)

When it comes to people outside the faith, whatever their
sexual orientation, we're called to talk about *and embody*
the love of Jesus. The good news of Jesus Christ is not
about sin management. Think about it. *Even if* you were
able to convince someone to stop sleeping around—
assuming, of course, that they're sleeping around—
abstinence won't save them. We're not saved by sexual
purity, but by the purifying work of Christ.

Gospel first. Sexuality later.

The beauty of this perspective is that it forces us to *trust
the power of the gospel*. It's easy to look at life through
human lenses, so that we feel
as if everyone's salvation is
up to us, and we frantically
search for ways to squeeze
our unbelieving friends into
the kingdom. But God is the
one who saves and sanctifies.

For a discussion about the centrality of the gospel in sexuality discussions, see the *Grace/Truth* podcast "The Gospel and Sexuality."

Ultimately, it's not up to us to get people saved, and
it's not under our power to make sure everyone lives a
holy life. We are mediators in God's world to help God's

people. Sometimes we screw up. (No, *oftentimes* we screw up.) We treat our friends poorly, fail to witness to our neighbors, and when it comes to parenting—God help us all!

We are fragile players in a game of redemption, always and everywhere in need of God's grace. It's the *gospel*, not our efforts, that saves. And it's the same *gospel* that sanctifies. Trust in the power of the gospel to do the impossible.

One of my friends left his wife for a relationship with a man after eighteen years of marriage. He was married to his new husband for four years but then divorced him for yet another man. After sixteen years of living with his new partner, they both woke up one day and said, "I think we're living in sin. We should repent and follow Jesus." And so they stopped their sexual relationship and started following Jesus passionately and consistently.

No words, no sermons, no picketers, no gospel tracts. Just Jesus—unmediated. God broke into the lives of this gay couple and brought them to himself through repentance and faith. They weren't eased into the kingdom. They were drop-kicked.

This isn't always the way it works. Sometimes people come to Christ through hours and hours of conversations with other Christians. But the one thing every Christian has in common is this: it's the power of the gospel that got them there.

## 4. Don't Be a Hypocrite

One of the biggest barriers between LGBT+ people and the church is religious hypocrisy among Christians. We're seen as being soft on divorce, greed, gluttony, and sexual sins committed by straight people, while eagerly condemning same-sex sexual sins.

The fact is: *We Christians tend to vilify the sins we're least likely to commit.* And this has been a massive problem among straight Christians. If we expelled from church everyone who engages in fornication, unbiblical divorces, adultery, porn, greed, pride, materialism, and gluttony, we might as well close the doors of the church and turn it into a nightclub. And yet we've been quick to judge gay people.

So you can imagine why LGBT+ people, most of whom grew up in church, are bitter about the hypocrisy among straight Christians. We tend to judge LGBT+ people while ignoring our own sins.

The book of John tells a beautiful story about a woman caught in adultery (John 8:1–11). She's dragged out by the religious leaders, who are ready to stone her when Jesus jumps to her defense and says, "Let any one of you who is without sin be the first to throw a stone at her" (8:7 NIV). He wasn't defending her sin—Jesus is quite clear about what he thinks of adultery. But he stood against the hypocrisy of the religious leaders. They were ready to deal with someone else's sin without dealing with their own.

> We Christians tend to vilify the sins we're least likely to commit.

It's a beautiful story, celebrated by Christians. But you need to ask yourself: if the religious leaders brought forth a gay man who'd just had sex with another man, would you be there with Jesus, on the side of the gay man, or standing with the Pharisees with a handful of stones?

## 5. Don't Be Afraid to Say "I'm Sorry"

In 2015, I published a book on homosexuality titled *People to Be Loved: Why Homosexuality Is Not Just an Issue*. Before its release, I was getting a lot of flak on social media for writing on the topic. Despite the title, there were some people who were angry that another straight, white, evangelical male was writing on this topic. I even heard someone say, "Preston needs to realize that we're not just some issue; we're *people!*" (I couldn't help but chuckle, "Have you at least read the title?") So what did I do? Well, I fired off an aggressive blog that defended myself and my reasons for writing the book. As expected, the blogosphere looked like I had swatted the hornet's nest. Vitriolic blogs attacking my post swirled through the internet. Even my close friends, who agree with my position, said my blog felt more arrogant and angry than they're used to seeing from me. So what did I do?

Well, after praying and seeking counsel from several godly friends, I wrote a follow-up post titled "An Apology." I didn't defend myself. I just apologized. I didn't apologize for my theological views or for being a white, straight, evangelical man. But I did apologize for the tone in which I had voiced my views. I apologized for specific things I said and the way I said them.

Even though my apology this time swatted the conservative hornet's nest—they thought I was caving into "those homosexuals" and affirming "the gay lifestyle"—I actually shocked a lot of LGBT+ people looking on. Quite a few of them said, "We've never seen an evangelical leader apologize before."

While I was encouraged by their response, it was a sad commentary on the evangelical church. *Never seen an evangelical leader apologize before?* Isn't that what it means to be a Christian—to publicly confess our sin and acknowledge our imperfections? Several LGBT+ people who were very turned off by my original post were so surprised by my apology that they were now very interested in reading my book on homosexuality—a book that clearly and thoroughly articulates a traditional view of Christian sexuality.

Many Christians have made mistakes in this conversation; few have apologized. And people know it. Don't be afraid to apologize for the mistakes you may have made. If you have a gay relative, friend, neighbor, or coworker, and they've been jaded by the church and are bitter toward Christianity, don't be afraid to apologize. You don't need to say, "I'm sorry for my beliefs" or "I'm sorry for Christianity's view of marriage." But if you say, "I'm sorry for how some Christians have mistreated LGBT+ people—it really breaks my heart," you'll probably pave a relational highway that could lead to redemption. If your gay son or daughter or grandkid has had a bad experience in the church, don't get all defensive. They probably *have* had a legitimately bad experience—no excuses! A simple apology shows empathy and concern, humility and grace. Even if you weren't responsible for their experience (and maybe you did play a role), an apology shows that you at least care and want to create a better church environment.

An apology demonstrates humility and it confronts pride. It tells the world that you don't have it all figured out and you don't want to hurt people. It lets people know that you're not perfect—only Jesus is. And whenever Jesus' perfection is put on display, that's a beautiful thing. You never need to apologize for holding on to a traditional, Christian ethic of sexuality and gender. But there's a chance that the manner and tone of your belief has hurt someone who's gay.

## 6. Be a Safe Person

Most non-Christian LGBT+ people grew up in the church (83 percent according to one study).[1] Think about it. This means that the future members and leaders of the LGBT+ community are today's church-going youth. Many of them hide their sexuality and gender struggles. They're lonely, isolated, and scared to talk to their leaders. Why?

Because they don't view their leaders as safe people to talk to.

Maybe they're right, or maybe their fears are unfounded. Maybe their leaders would receive their struggle with kindness and care. Either way, our struggling youth don't get the vibe that their leaders are safe people to talk to. The "loud and proud" anti-Christian LGBT+ activist may never come to your church. But God forgive us if we ever cause the silent and scared to leave because they felt unsafe or unloved.

Laurie, whom you've met in the videos, grew up in the church and didn't tell anyone about her struggle with same-sex attraction. Why? Because she didn't view others around her as safe people to talk to. If a leader told a gay joke, or laughed at a gay joke, or used phrases like *those homosexuals* or *the gay lifestyle*, they were seen as unsafe to talk to. Their language, posture, and tone revealed that they probably wouldn't respond well to a gay kid coming out, and so Laurie just kept smiling and doing her Christian thing, all the while being tormented by her struggles with sexuality.

Most likely, the people around her meant no harm. They weren't intentionally trying to push her away. They didn't even know she was struggling! But that's sort of the point. They *could have* known about her struggle if they had proven to be safe to talk to. They *could have* mediated the love of Jesus to this young Jesus follower struggling with her sexuality if they had given the impression that they were safe.

What does it mean to be a safe person? Exhibiting public kindness. Showing love toward the marginalized and outsiders. Demonstrating that you listen deeply to what people are actually saying. Not being judgmental and condemning. Embodying the radical grace of Christ. Showing public and courageous concern for LGBT+ people—despite what other people may think. And, of course, never telling or laughing at a gay joke.

These are the trademarks of a safe person. Are you a safe person?

// // //

Throughout this conversation, I've been talking about LGBT+ people in general. I haven't always made a distinction between Christian and non-Christian LGBT+ people. The fact is, even conservative same-sex attracted Christians often feel a relational chill from straight Christians and constantly wonder what place they have in the church. Therefore, the relational principles above apply to all gay/straight relations, regardless of faith commitment.

However, there are several important questions we've yet to address head on. *How should the church relate to affirming LGBT+ people who confess the name of Jesus? Should they be accepted or confronted, welcomed or kicked out of the church?* Or to take my example above: *Should we "listen, learn, and listen again" to LGBT+ people who say they're following Christ and are also engaging in sexually immoral behavior? Or should we listen, learn, and then challenge them to repent?*

These are all important questions, and we'll address them in *Grace/Truth 2.0*.

## QUESTIONS FOR DISCUSSION

1. Why do you think that Christians haven't had the best reputation for being good listeners in conversations about sexuality and gender?

2. Describe an experience in which you shared something intimate with a friend or family member, and they listened intently and authentically. Have you had the opposite experience, where someone clearly wasn't listening with compassion? How did these experiences make you feel?

3. Have you ever seen the gospel work in powerful ways in the life of a person of whom you'd least expect it? Describe this experience.

4. Reflect on this statement: "We weren't commissioned to preach a gospel of 'Don't have gay sex' but rather 'Believe on the Lord Jesus and you will be saved.'" Do you agree with this? Why or why not? Do you have any questions related to this statement?

5. Along with phrases like *the gay lifestyle* or *the gay agenda*, are there other words or phrases that you think might offend LGBT+ people?

6. Do you think that same-sex sexual behavior is a worse sin than other sins? Why or why not?

7. Do you feel that the charge of hypocrisy made against Christians is accurate? Why or why not? In what ways have you experienced more consistency among Christians in how they view sins other than same-sex sexual behavior that they don't necessarily struggle with?

8. When you were a high-school student, would you have felt comfortable "coming out" to your parents? If you are a parent, do you believe your children would confide in you? Why or why not?

9. What is likely to happen if a high-school student in your church, who's attracted to the same sex, goes off to college or the workplace without talking to a trusted adult? Do you know what your church is doing to walk with them and prepare them to face the unique challenges they will encounter?

10. Can you remember a time when your genuine apology helped restore a relationship with someone (they don't have to be LGBT+)? Or a time when someone offended you and their apology restored the relationship? Please describe.

11. Do you feel like you're a safe person for an LGBT+ Christian to talk to? Why or why not? How do you think you could improve in this area?

## CHAPTER ENDNOTE

1 Andrew Marin, *Us Versus Us: The Untold Story of Religion and the LGBT Community* (Colorado Springs: NavPress, 2016).

# Conclusion

I hope you've enjoyed—or at least feel that you've gained insight from—our five conversations on faith, sexuality, and gender. We tried to address some of the most important topics and answer the most frequently asked questions in the LGBT+ discussion. But I'm sure that you have many questions that weren't addressed, and our conversations probably unearthed several other questions you didn't even know you had. That's okay. It's expected, actually. The more I dig into LGBT+ related issues, the more I discover that there is so much more I can learn.

And that's why we created *Grace/Truth 2.0: Five More Conversations about Faith, Sexuality & Gender that Every Thoughtful Christian Should Have*. This second study dives deeper into questions related to gender, transgender, and intersex, along with addressing several other affirming arguments that we didn't get into in *Grace/Truth 1.0*. We also pay special attention to ministry-related questions that Christian leaders often ask, so if you are a leader (or simply an interested lay person with unanswered questions!) I encourage you to go through *Grace/Truth 2.0*.

Throughout this study, we've considered two main ideas: *grace* and *truth*.

*Grace* emphasizes loving people who fall short of the truth—which, if I were to guess, includes *all* of us. Whether we're gay or straight, we've all been made crooked by the Fall and by the sinful choices in our own lives. So if you celebrate God's grace showered upon you—a sexually broken sinner—then you should courageously embody this same love toward others.

*Truth* focuses on what the Bible says about marriage and sexuality. God created marriage to be a one-flesh union between two sexually different persons, and all sexual acts outside of this union are sin. If the same God who breathed stars into existence also breathed out the words in Scripture that give us guidance on sexuality and marriage, then we should walk faithfully according to God's direction.